LIFE & LOSS

A Guide to Help Grieving Children

Linda Goldman

ACCELERATED DEVELOPMENT
A member of the Taylor & Francis Group

LIFE & LOSS
A Guide to Help Grieving Children

Technical Development: Cynthia Long
Marguerite Mader
Sheila Sheward

Cover Design: Arthur Goldberg

Library of Congress Cataloging-in-Publication Data

Goldman, Linda, 1946-
Life & loss : a guide to help grieving children / Linda Goldman.
p.   cm.
Includes bibliographical references and index.
ISBN 1-55959-052-1
1. Grief in children.   2. Loss (Psychology) in children.
3. Children--Counseling of.   I. Title.   II. Title: Life and loss.
BF723.G75G65   1994
155.4'12--dc20   93-29333
CIP

LCN: 93-29333
ISBN: 1-55959-052-1

Order Additional Copies From

ACCELERATED DEVELOPMENT
A member of the Taylor & Francis Group
1900 Frost Road, Suite 101, Bristol, PA 19007-1598
1-800-821-8312

This book is dedicated to the children of the world and to the child within each of us.

When anecdotes appear throughout the guide, the names and particular incidents have been modified to maintain the privacy of the people in the stories. The people in the photographs are not related to the material on the page on which they appear.

PREFACE

The 90s is the information age, overflowing with instant communication. We are inundated with losses through TV, movies, newspapers, videos, and computers. Mass media make available at lightening speed any issue that exists on earth today. Our world is shrinking. What's happening in the inner cities affects the suburbs. What's happening in Russia affects the U.S. What's happening on Wall Street affects the grocery store. What's happening in government affects our schools. What's happening within our minds affects our children.

> ### Let's meet today's world—today's needs—today's children—with a new way of seeing.

Mass communication, often shocking in content, has created instantly a global group therapy process. Our ideas, thoughts, and feelings immediately are pooled, shared, and projected into the light of day for all to see and hear. We continually are made aware of each other's issues and, therefore, our own. We no longer can deny the hidden **parts of ourselves.** When we watched the police beating Rodney King, or later the L.A. rioters, were we not also watching **parts of ourselves?** Perhaps it seemed so horrible because it touched the prejudice, fear, rage, and shame in all of us. The adult generation of the 90s was raised on fear, guilt, and denial. We only recently are beginning to come to terms with our own childhood issues, which assuredly will help us help our children come to terms with their own.

The potential for healing is boundless. As we explode the tendency to perceive our issues as our own private embarrassments, we open the path of joining with each other to work through our pain. This ability to share our private worlds openly, whether on Oprah, in *People* magazine, or on Sesame Street, lessens everyone's need for denial. Our inner strength is released as a powerful tool, offering potential for change and personal growth.

But there is a problem. Denial, fear, shame, and lack of appropriate role models shaped the lives of most adults. This often makes it difficult for us to relate to children with innocence, simplicity, and openness, especially in the sensitive area of loss and grief. Yet, children are being immersed constantly in this ever changing open environment and need grown-ups to serve as role models for them. Parents, educators, and other caring professionals have the responsibility of helping these kids with their grief process. This guide has been written to serve as a role model. Through the use of photographs, children's work, anecdotes, simple techniques, and resources, we can "tune in" to the world of children. **Hopefully this book will help unlock the door of respect for the child's inner universe and offer the key to enter into it with integrity.**

INTRODUCTION

This book is written for and about children. It is also written for and about adults who want to help kids work through their issues of loss and grief. As a mom, stepmother, teacher, counselor, and educator, I am very aware of the importance of open communication, expression of feelings, and helpful resources during sensitive times in a child's life. My goal is to create a guide that empowers parents, educators, clergy, and health care professionals to handle children's loss and grief issues in an informed, open, and loving way, reducing fear and denial often associated with these topics.

> **Each chapter of this guide includes suggestions that allow the mind, the heart, and common sense to work together to create a caring environment for kids.**

This guide is user friendly. One can open to any page and find useful information. Pictures are placed throughout the book as a reminder of the child's world and ways for adults to enter into it. The reader may be surprised to see so many photographs showing children in a light- hearted fashion. These pictures illustrate how much time children spend with play and fantasy, no matter what their life circumstances or inner feelings may be. An active, playing child can still be a grieving child. Children escape and deny just as adults do. Yet children's form for working through much of their grief is play.

I have chosen to use real-life ancedotes that illustrate typical situations. Each story is followed by a section with practical ideas on how to help a child understand each situation and adjust to the change. Ways to prepare for grief, resources to use, and follow-up activites are included. **This simplified but structured approach is beneficial in working with a wide range of circumstances.** The basic ideas can be modified and expanded to fit new challenges that arise in the life of a child.

I have chosen the title, *LIFE AND LOSS: A Guide to Help Grieving Children*, for many reasons. While we need to recognize death as an important part of life, it is one of many losses children experience. Whether it be a broken toy, a broken leg, a broken home, or a broken heart, children grieve and mourn. Moving, divorce, abuse, and illness are issues interwoven into the threads of grief work that exist side by side with the death of a loved one (pet, friend, neighbor, sibling, parent, or grandparent).

In the first chapter, the stage of understanding is set by providing loss and grief statistics in the 90s. It explores the categories of childhood losses and offers suggestions on how to help. The remaining chapters develop a deeper understanding of concepts that underlie Chapter 1.

The myths of loss and grief with which we as caring adults have been reared and pass on to our children are explored in Chapter 2. We need to acknowledge these myths and replace them with fact.

The four psychological tasks of grief are explained in Chapter 3. Material is presented to provide an understanding of each task. Limiting cliches are replaced by more appropriate responses. The child's developmental understanding from birth to adolescence is viewed. Ways to commemorate are offered. The story of Star, a pet dog that has died, offers practical ideas for real-life situations.

Grief resolution techniques that can be used at home, in school, or on the playground are presented in Chapter 4. Identifying behaviors associated with grief and loss is the first step in working actively with children's needs. Then we can use storytelling, letter writing, drama, artwork, music, and crafts to stimulate and expand discussions with children.

Chapter 5 is a special story that provides a needed answer to the question of what to say and what to do when a child wants to say goodbye to a dying person. Through one mother's eyes, we learn a world of knowledge and broaden the ideas to include a general format for other loss and grief issues.

Chapter 6 is especially for educators. It describes the challenges they and their students face daily. Guidelines for educational referrals and a children's loss inventory are included. Practical ways to use teachable moments in the classroom are described.

Chapter 7 contains a list of national resources that can be helpful to adults working with children. A general list of community resources that caregivers can pursue is included to help in establishing a community networking system.

An exploration of materials is possible through Chapter 8, where annotations are included with books for adults and children, videos, manuals, guides, and curricula. Children's literature is divided into categories according to the loss issue. Age appropriateness is considered throughout.

TABLE OF CONTENTS

Chapter 1

CHILDREN'S LOSS AND GRIEF

DEATH   DRUGS   DIVORCE

ILLNESS   UNEMPLOYMENT   AIDS   ABUSE

POLLUTION   TERRORISM   HOMELESSNESS

NATURAL DISASTERS   VIOLENCE

THAT'S WHAT'S THE MATTER WITH KIDS TODAY

WHAT'S THE MATTER WITH KIDS TODAY?

We asked ourselves, "What's the matter with kids today?" and discovered it is the answer; it is not the question. It is the answer because the very need to ask that question is an indication of adult denial. Adults asking the question have created this grief-filled world, and the children are confronted with it's fear and chaos.

Donna O'Toole, children's grief educator and author of *Growing through Grief* (1989), warned that "Too often they are the forgotten ones, lacking role models and assurances for a safe journey, they accumulate losses—attaching themselves to their memories," and literally can be left "frozen in time and buried alive in inner space" if they don't have the opportunity to work out their feelings.

We ask ourselves, "What's the matter with kids today?" The answer is that the world is different than the one in which we grew up.

Today's children witness violence daily. A little boy asked his school teacher who George Washington was. "He was our first President" was the reply. "Who shot him?" he asked, automatically assuming all presidents get shot.

In a 1992 movie, "Grand Canyon," a teenager involved in gang violence was asked by his uncle, " Why are you doing this? What will you do when you're 20?" "Are you kidding me?" the teenager said. "I'll be dead by 20."

TODAY'S FACTS ABOUT CHILDREN'S GRIEF

Today's children are confronted by a set of experiences and memories largely incomprehensible to us.

DEATH

Twelve percent of all childhood deaths are caused by guns in accidents, suicides, and murders. Eleven children a day are killed.

Auto accidents are the leading cause of accidental deaths of children. Drownings are second.

In a school system of 6,000 students, an average of four students die a year.

Twenty percent of today's children will have experienced the death of a parent by the end of high school.

DIVORCE

Over 6 million children are living in divorced families. One- third will lose contact with one parent.

Fifty percent of today's children will experience parental divorce by the end of high school.

SEXUAL ABUSE

One out of three girls are sexually abused by age 18.
One out of seven boys are sexually abused by age 18.

RELOCATION

Today's children will have experienced an average of four moves per family by the end of high school.

EXPOSURE TO VIOLENCE

The estimate is that a child by age 14 will witness 18,000 deaths (usually violent murders) on TV.

Sources: Donna O'Toole, *Growing through Grief* (1989);
Alan Wolfelt, *Centerpiece* (Summer, 1992);
Victor S. & Edith Lombardo, *Kids Grieve Too* (1986).

What Can We Do for the Child?

We can help the child by first helping ourselves. Our honesty in seeing and relaying loss and grief issues that run through our lives will indeed be the role model for our children. By networking with other caring adults and using the many resources available, we can minimize our fear and denial and create an environment in which children know their own strength and power from facing and working through their pain.

Developing your psychological strength is just like developing physical abilities. The more you exercise, the stronger you become.

Harold Bloomfield and Leonard Felder
<u>Achilles Syndrome</u>
New York: Random House 1986

CHILDHOOD LOSS

I have come to see that all hurt and pain is based on tangible and intangible losses. From the loss of a child's tooth to the death of a parent, we grieve what we miss and want back—whether it be a mom, a pet, a toy, or our dignity and respect. Childhood losses can fall into one of the following categories (O'Toole, 1989).

Relationships   External Objects   The Environment
Self   Skills/Ability   Habits

LOSS OF RELATIONSHIPS

Death of a parent, grandparent, sibling, friend, classmate, pet
Absence of teacher, parent, sibling, friend
Unavailability of parent due to alcoholism, drugs, imprisonment, divorce

The death of a pet can be a significant loss in a child's life. Ellen, age 9, loved her dog very much. Buffy was Ellen's friend and companion. She fed him, brushed him, walked with him, and talked with him. During the school day, Buffy got hit by a car and killed. A neighbor, out of kindness, took Buffy's body to the vet so that Ellen wouldn't have to see it. She never got to say good-bye. "It's only a dog," her parents said. "We'll get you another one."

There was no other dog for Ellen. She loved Buffy and he was gone. Deeply mourning his loss for years to come, Ellen continued to carry this grief because she had no environment in which to mourn openly.

Sam loved his dog too. Sam played ball with Charlie every day after school. Charlie was a problem pet. Because Charlie was never completely housebroken or disciplined, Sam's parents made several unsuccessful attempts to sell Charlie or give him away. One day Sam came home from school. His dog was gone. Sam's parents said they gave Charlie to a good home. Sam questioned the truth of that explanation. No one had ever wanted to take Charlie before. The facts of his disappearance haunted Sam through his teenage years. Was Charlie killed? Was he abandoned? Was he hurt? Where did he go?

What Can We Do for the Child?

1. Tell the child the truth about the pet's death or other events surrounding the pet's leaving.

2. Allow the child to see the pet after it has died if the body is relatively intact. It helps to make the death real.

3. Have a funeral and burial for the pet when possible. If pets are too large to bury, or a backyard is too small, a memorial service is an appropriate ritual.   Let the child have a part in creating it.

4. Acknowledge children's memories and encourage them to talk about their pet.

5. Encourage children to express feelings. Express your own.

6. Be aware of the child's guilty feelings that in some way the death or disappearance of the pet was the child's fault. (Why didn't I stay home from school that day? Why did I let my dog go outside?) Discuss ways the child was good to his or her pet. Discuss regrets too.

7. Use rituals to work through grief. Look at photos.   Write down feelings and memories.   Draw a picture for or of the pet. Save a special object (collar or ball) in a special place.

8. Have parents inform the school. Have educators let the child know they care. Use discussions as a teachable moment in school.

Network: Use a support system of people who understand the depth of grief involving pet loss (family, friends, veterinarians).

Call *Pet Loss Hotline* at (916) 752-4200 Monday through Friday.

Resources

Jim's Dog Muffin
    by Miriam Cohen
    (1984)

About Dying
    by Sarah Stein
    (1974)

When a Pet Dies
    by Fred Rogers
    (1988)

It Must Hurt a Lot
    by Doris Sanford (1985a)

LOSS OF EXTERNAL OBJECTS

> **Loss of favorite toy or object**
> **(blanket, pacifier, teddy bear)**
> **Loss through robbery or being misplaced**
> **(diary, special gift)**

Nancy always traveled with Lizzie, her favorite stuffed koala bear. When Nancy visited Grandma, slept over at friends, or traveled with her family, Lizzie was the first thing Nancy packed. Her family's trip to San Francisco proved traumatic. After the first night in a fine hotel, Nancy and her parents went out to explore the city. Returning at bedtime they discovered Lizzie was gone. They searched and searched. Nancy cried and cried. "How can I sleep without Lizzie," she wept. "I want to go home."

What Can We Do for the Child?

1. Validate her deep feelings for her stuffed animal as a truly important companion.

2. Actively share in the search for the stuffed animal.

3. Actively employ a self-help group. The hotel staff searched and searched for Lizzie. Two days later Lizzie was found in their laundry room. A little cleaner, a little shrunken, and ever ready to be held and loved again.

Resources

A Bunch of Balloons
    by Dorothy Ferguson
    (1992)

The Fall of Freddie the Leaf
    by Leo Buscaglia (1982)

I Know I Made It Happen
    by Lynn Blackburn (1991)

> **Fire, floods, hurricanes and other natural disasters**
> **Moving, changing school, changing family structure**
> **Family separation**

Family separation can be a painful grieving process for a young child. Whether it is leaving Mom to stay with a baby-sitter, parents going on a trip, or a grandmother dying, the loss is real and important.

When my little boy Jonathan was 5, I went away for six days. When I came back I asked him how it was for him when I was gone. He said, "Well, I got a little angry when people kept asking where you were, and Mom, what does unbearable mean?" I said "Something really hard to take." He replied, "It was unbearable!"

What Can We Do for the Child?

1. Prepare the child for the parent's leaving. Whether a parent leaves for an hour, a day, a week, indefinitely, or forever, the child needs to know the facts. Open discussion decreases anxiety.

2. Make a calendar with the child showing how long Mom will be away. Leave it in his/her room. The child can mark off the days.

3. Leave a picture of the parent by the child's bed.

4. Use a tape recorder for the child to talk to the parent or work out feelings about the parent leaving.

5 Leave the phone number of a caring adult who can support the child.

6. Inform the teacher about what has happened or will be happening at home.

Resources

The Good-Bye Book
    by Judith Viorst (1992)
About Change and Moving
    by Joy Berry (1990)
Please Come Home
    by Doris Sanford (1985b)
My Daddy Takes Care of Me
    by Patricia Quinlin (1987)

LOSS OF SELF

Loss of physical part of the body: tooth, arm, eye

Loss of self-esteem: physical, sexual, emotional or deprivational abuse

---

Behavioral symptoms of grief are not always fighting and crying or other outer expressions. Children can withdraw, detach, and depersonalize life to escape issues of grief so painful that not feeling and not talking are the only ways to survive.

This is what Mary had to do. Her dad had committed suicide when she was 5. Never told the facts, she was informed that he died in an accident. Taken from her natural mother and not told why (although Mary later discovered that Mom was an alcoholic), Mary went to live with an aunt and uncle. Mary was extremely withdrawn in school. No one asked why. Her uncle had been sexually abusing her from age 5 through age 9. She became more and more withdrawn. No one asked why—not at school, not at church, not her friends' parents, not the community. At age 9, Mary began to talk and began begging not to be left alone with her uncle. She was punished inappropriately and told she was unappreciative.

Where are the adults, the advocates, the voices for the withdrawn children who carry the emotional pain of loss and grief that is so heavy and so filled with fear and abandonment that their silent cries scream to be heard by someone who can help?

Let's open our inner ears to the quiet of the voiceless children. Let's hear their pain with our hearts.

Mary quietly withdrew, becoming shy and unapproachable. She seemed to internalize her problems of dealing with adults. When she bravely attempted to talk about her problems, they were denied by her adult world.

Mark, a 15-month-old, acted out his hurt in a different way to secure attention. Mark's mom asked what she could do for her son who was showing visible signs of distress after returning from visitations with his dad. The couple had divorced, partially due to the husband's alleged abusive nature. The child clung to Mom, cried a lot, had temper tantrums, and didn't want to be left alone. The court ruling had given the father two-day visitation rights, even though his abuse of his wife was on record. Mom also said she noticed a bruise on the child and was angry about it. "I know my husband hits Mark but I don't know what to do about it." **I didn't know either, but I decided to find out.**

For Mary and Mark, knowing the signs of abuse is the first step in confronting their abusive situations, whether the abuse is physical, sexual, or by neglect.

SIGNS OF ABUSE IN CHILDREN

With the help of Nancy Eike, director of N.W. Child Protective Network of the Omni Youth Service, I have adapted the following indicators of abuse in children. It is essential for parents, teachers, counselors, clergy, and pediatricians to watch for internal (verbal) or external (physical) signs . *If more than one* of the following signs are present, you need to report the suspected findings to the proper authorities. You should suspect abuse if a child

—is habitually away from school and constantly late;

—arrives at school very early and leaves very late because he or she does not want to go home;

—is compliant, shy, withdrawn, passive, and uncommunicative;

—is nervous, hyperactive, aggressive, disruptive, or destructive;

—has an unexplained injury—a patch of hair missing, a burn, a limp, or bruises;

—has an inappropriate number of "unexplained" injuries such as bruises on his or her arms or legs over a period of time;

—exhibits an injury that is not adequately explained;

—complains about numerous beatings;

—complains about the mother's boyfriend "doing things" when the mother is not home;

—goes to the bathroom with difficulty;

—is dressed inadequately for inclement weather;

—wears a long sleeved blouse or shirt during the summer to cover bruises on the arms;

—has clothing that is soiled, tattered, or too small;

—is dirty and smells or has bad teeth, hair falling out, or lice;

—is thin, emaciated, and constantly tired, showing evidence of malnutrition and dehydration;

—is usually fearful of other children and adults;

—has been given inappropriate food, drink, or drugs; and/or

—talks about someone touching private parts.

SIGNS OF ABUSIVE PARENTS

Child abuse should be suspected by any caring adult if the parents show *more than one* of the following:

—**show little concern for their child's problems;**

—**do not respond to the teacher's inquiries and are never present for parent's night or private teacher conferences;**

—**take an unusual amount of time to seek health care for the child;**

—**do not adequately explain an injury;**

—**give different explanations for the same injury;**

—**suggest that the cause of an injury can be attributed to a third party;**

—**are reluctant to share information about the child;**

—**respond inappropriately to the seriousness of the problem;**

—**cannot be found;**

—**are using alcohol or drugs;**

—**have no friends, relatives, or neighbors to turn to in times of crisis;**

—**have unrealistic expectations for the child;**

—**are very strict disciplinarians;**

—**were abused, neglected, or deprived themselves;**

—**have taken the child to different doctors, clinics, or hospitals for past injuries (possibly trying to cover up the fact of repeated injuries);**

—**show signs of loss of control or a fear of losing control; and/or**

—**are usually antagonistic and hostile when talking about the child's health problems.**

Nancy Eike emphasized that "these clues can help adults make an informed decision about reporting." **Educators** in particular are required only to report *suspected* abuse to the proper authorities. To investigate is the responsibility of the authorities. **Parents** can obtain supporting documentation from other official caregiving settings. No one needs to disclose his or her name when reporting suspected abuse to State Children's Protective Services. These services must "act" within 24 to 48 hours. They may not decide to take specific action to separate the child from the family. However, each report will add strength to the next one made about the same abuse case.

What Can We Do for the Child?

For children under 3, their primary needs are met by physical comforting such as hugging, holding, and permitting appropriate regression. Caregiving adults need guidance in working with their anger so that they become freer to love their child.

Doris Sanford is the author of *I Can't Talk about It*, an excellent book for children on sexual abuse. She stressed it is important to

1. **encourage no self blame,**
2. **encourage repetition of telling the story,**
3. **assure total belief of the abuse,**
4. **maintain privacy,**
5. **control your anger about the abuse,**
6. **offer protection,**
7. **remember sometimes there is no visible sign of abuse, and**
8. **acknowledge you feel bad about the abuse.**

"There is no place so potentially violent as home. It is sometimes a place of special betrayal because the child's guard is down. If you are abusing a child, please accept help. If you are being abused, tell someone and keep telling until you get the help you need."

Doris Sanford, *I Can't Talk about It.* (1986).
Portland, OR: Questar Publishers, Multnomah Press.

Resources

Helping Your Child Recover from Sexual Abuse
    by Caren Adams and Jennifer Fay (1992)

I Can't Talk about It
    by Doris Sanford (1986)

Something Is Wrong in My House
    by Diane Davis (1984)

LOSS RELATED TO SKILLS AND ABILITIES

> **Held back in school**
> **Not chosen for team sports**
> **Overweight, injured, illness, physical disability**
> **Dyslexia, ADHD, other developmental**
> **differences**

In my first year of teaching I was given a second grade class of 22 repeaters. We were placed in a trailer away from the school. Some of the children were labeled "slow learners"; others were on medication for ADHD (Attention Deficit Hyperactivity Disorder); still others just seemed to be neglected at home. The children began school with the shame and stigma of failing second grade individually and as a group. The humiliation extended to their physical isolation in the trailer. I looked at their faces the first day of class and saw a lack of joy and an aura of poor self-esteem. They knew they were different and felt the despair of their perceived lack of achievement.

What Can We Do for the Child?

1. Recognize facts about the child's school placement.
2. Allow children opportunities to discuss their retention openly.
3. Incorporate the children's thoughts and feelings into creative writing and language experience.
4. Accept the children for where they are academically by using classwork and homework geared to their level of ability and comfort. See growth as individually progressing and not just as standardized grade level comparisons of where children *should* be.
5. Create a project where the class can shine. Since the repeating second graders are a year older than the other second grade class, use the maturity in a creative way (plays, murals, school service projects).
6. Use every opportunity to encourage self-esteem. The following poem is a creative way (with a little humor) to bring home the point for adults and children that despite outward differences, we're all alike inside.

NO DIFFERENCE

Small as a peanut,
Big as a giant,
We're all the same size
When we turn off the light.

Rich as a sultan,
Poor as a mite,
We're all worth the same
When we turn off the light.

Red, black, or orange,
Yellow or white,
We all look the same
When we turn off the light.

So maybe the way
To make everything right
Is for someone to just reach out
And turn off the light!

From the book, *Where the Sidewalk Ends,* by Shel Silverstein

(Copyright 1974 by HarperCollins Publishers. Reprinted by permission.)

LOSS RELATED TO HABITS

**Sucking thumb, biting fingernails, twirling hair
Change in eating patterns or daily routines
Beginning school or ending school**

A bus accident on the way to school certainly can change the routine of the day for the children involved. This happened to a group of 25 elementary school children. Timmy was the only first grader among them. The bus swerved to avoid a truck and was thrown over on its side. Miraculously no one was severely hurt. The children waited for the police, were taken to the hospital in ambulances, and the parents were notified. The accident was a disturbing disruption to the school routine. Some kids were emotionally shaken. One child fainted. Other kids were bruised and cut. Timmy had a few scrapes on his face. He raced to his mom when she entered the hospital, hugged her tightly, and insisted in a frightened voice, "I'm never riding the bus again, and you can't make me!"

What Can We Do for the Child?

1. Bring children together to discuss feelings about the bus accident experience. Listen and echo back feelings.

2. Allow each child the time and space to retell his/her version of the story. This helps to see where support or clarification is needed.

3. Let each child mark on a diagram of the bus where he or she was sitting and tell what he or she did.

4. Recognize any injuries that the children sustained.

5. Discuss guilt that some children may feel if they were one of the ones not injured.

6. Identify the fears for future bus rides. Reassure that everything has been done to insure safety.

7. Bring the entire school together for an assembly. Discuss what an accident is and the facts surrounding the bus accident. Allow all children time for questions. This will respond to the needs of the school children who were not on the bus.

8. Inform parents of all the children in the school. Send home the facts of the accident and how it has been handled with their children.

9. Listen, and respond with care, because children often refer to their scary experience in their talk or play for many months after the accident. To do so is normal and healthy.

10. Have parents and teachers reassure children: **it was an accident, no one was hurt seriously, and we are all OK.**

**HUMAN BEINGS AND ESPECIALLY CHILDREN
CAN SURVIVE VERY FRIGHTENING
EXPERIENCES**

Network

1. Set up a telephone network for the kids who were on the bus to call each other and share their feelings.

2. Set up a time during school where these kids who were in the accident can continue to share their feelings.

Resources

Alexander and the Terrible Horrible No Good Very Bad Day
by Judith Viorst (1972)

Don't Pop Your Cork on Monday by Adolph Moser (1988)

About Traumatic Experiences by Joy Berry (1990)

Chapter 2

MYTHS OF GRIEF

"You'll get over it."
"Crying won't help."
"Be strong for your mom."
"It's time to move on."
"You're too young to understand."

COMMON MYTHS ABOUT LOSS AND GRIEF

1. Grief and mourning are the same experience.

2. Adults instantly can give explanations to children about death and spirituality.

3. The experience of grief and mourning has orderly stages.

4. The grief of adults does not impact on the bereaved child.

5. Adults should avoid topics that cause a child to cry.

6. An active playing child is not a grieving child.

7. Infants and toddlers are too young to grieve.

8. Parents, educators, and clergy always are prepared and qualified to give explanations and clarifications regarding loss and grief.

9. Children need to "get over" their grief and move on.

10. Children are better off not attending funerals.

> **If a child is old enough to love,
> he or she is old enough to grieve.**

(Adapted from Alan Wolfelt, author of *Helping Children Cope with Grief*, 1983.)

MYTHS OF LOSS AND GRIEF

We ask ourselves, "What's the matter with kids today?" and we answer, "They are being reared on the same myths of grief on which we were reared when we were young."

MYTH: GRIEF AND MOURNING ARE THE SAME.

Grief is defined as a normal, internalized reaction to the loss of a person, thing, or idea. It is our emotional response to loss.

Bereavement is the state of having lost something, whether it be significant others, significant things, or our sense of self. This state can range from the death of a parent, to the destruction of a home, to the loss of dreams, dignity, and self-respect.

Mourning means taking the internal experience of grief and expressing it outside of ourselves. It is the cultural expression of grief, as seen in traditional or creative rituals. Traditional rituals refer to ones that are sanctioned culturally, such as funerals. Creative rituals can be writing a letter to the deceased and then destroying it. Rituals are the behaviors we use to do grief work.

The story of Nicholas illustrates how a child's grief and mourning greatly affects his life. Nicholas' mourning became a burden to the school. He began acting out in school, fighting with friends, using bad language, writing graffiti wherever he could, failing school work, and complaining of stomach aches. The private school that Nicholas attended had little tolerance for his behaviors and asked him to leave, even though he had been there from kindergarten until eighth grade.

Many times bereaved children mourn through behaviors rather than words. Nicholas was mourning the loss of his family unit. His parents were getting divorced, and the situation was further compounded by his school abandoning him. Nicholas clearly exhibited behaviors to watch for in grieving children. These include anxiety, hostility towards others, and bodily distress. Had the educators in his school looked at his behaviors in a different way, the system may not have failed. Nicholas was an "unrecognized mourner." He was grieving but was not given the appropriate conditions to mourn in order to work out his feelings of loss.

In yesterday's world, Nicholas' acting out in school might have been the worst that could have happened. In today's world, another Nicholas may have just as easily brought a loaded pistol and shot a teacher or classmate, or turned to escapism through drugs or even suicide.

MYTH: ADULTS SHOULD INSTANTLY BE ABLE TO TEACH CHILDREN ABOUT DEATH AND SPIRITUALITY.

It's OK to admit we don't know all the answers—and not feel guilty that we can't define God in heaven or what happens after death. **LIFE AND DEATH CAN BE MYSTERIES.** A good example to illustrate to young children that sometimes things are a larger picture than we can always see and understand is the book, *Look Again*, by Tana Hoban (1971). Using smaller parts of a larger photograph, children can see there is a much larger picture than they possibly could have imagined.

MYTH: THE CHILD'S EXPERIENCE OF GRIEF IS A STAGE-LIKE PROGRESSION.

The concept of stages of grief often is misunderstood to be progressive and alike for everyone in every way. Grief work is unique to every adult and every child. Each person approaches it in his or her own way and at his or her own pace.

No two people are alike and neither is their grief.

An attitude that allows the child to be the true expert is one that says, "Teach me about your grief and I will be with you." We must remind ourselves not to prescribe how children should grieve and mourn, but allow them to teach us where they are in the process.

Two sons had very different reactions to their mother's cancer, chemotherapy, and loss of hair. The oldest, a pre- adolescent, was very embarrassed and refused to share his feelings. When he first saw his mom in a wig, he threw a towel over his head and ran out of the room. The youngest boy, a six-year-old, talked about his feelings a lot. Yet, he still had many nightmares. His teacher later shared that he had been writing a story in an ongoing journal every month about his baby-sitter who was very sick and eventually died. We can ask ourselves how we would treat these children by knowing their age level and what they told us about their process.

MYTH: THE GRIEF OF ADULTS DOES NOT IMPACT ON THE BEREAVED CHILD.

Parents, teachers, and adult friends are significant models for children. How adults mourn sets an example for surrounding children. If adults deny their grief, the children probably will do the same. If adults allow themselves to be sad or angry, it gives permission for the children to be sad or angry. Often adults try to hide their feelings from kids, falsely believing it is for their best interest. The guilt that a child may feel after someone he or she loves has left (as in divorce or moving) or died (due to an accident or illness) can be acknowledged and released if adult modeling allows for expression of feelings.

> **By allowing ourselves to mourn, we help the bereaved child to mourn.**

Another aspect of adult mourning negatively affecting children is the absence of the grieving parent emotionally and perhaps physically as well. This is a secondary loss for kids. Many times the caregiving parent is so distraught that he or she too is missing for the child for a period of time. It's a good idea to provide kids with a caring adult who can be a support system until the grieving parent has worked out some of his or her pain.

MYTH: ADULTS SHOULD AVOID TOPICS THAT CAUSE A CHILD TO CRY.

Jeff, a second grader, began acting out in school.   He began being very demanding of his friends, requiring extreme loyalty from them, needing to be boss at all times, and ultimately rejecting their friendship. His teacher talked to him several times about friendship and what he needed to do to be a good friend.   After many conversations, Jeff burst into tears. "Well, all my friends have left me," he sobbed. Crying was Jeff's way of relieving his tension and communicating his hurt and need to be comforted. It turned out that his four best friends had left his school at the end of first grade. He was mourning their loss and working out his feelings of abandonment. His teacher did many good things to help Jeff heal. She trusted her instincts and initiated a discussion with Jeff, even though he had not brought it up himself. She used his behaviors as a sign of grief, rather than a threat. She gave his loss validity and encouraged classmates to be a new support system for him.

Jeff's teacher led Jeff to realize he had a lot of good memories with his old friends and still could be with them even though they weren't at school. Jeff called his old friends and reestablished their relationship for after school time. He began to be less demanding of school friends. Jeff's teacher did not continue the myth that children need to be brave. Rather, she consciously did not avoid the painful topic that caused Jeff to cry, and helped Jeff get in touch with his pain and ultimately overcome it.

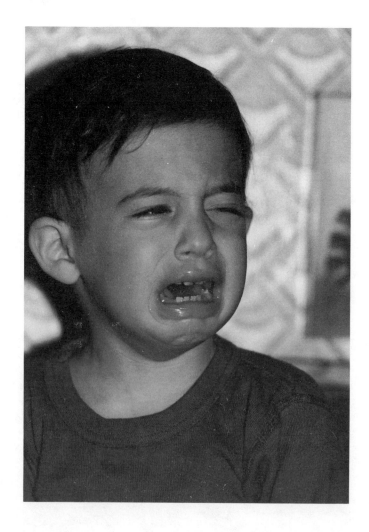

Jim was sad too. His Dad was in intensive care after his heart attack. He was told, "You need to be strong for your Mom," "Tears won't make him well," and "He wouldn't want you to cry." Unfortunately many adults associate tears of grief with personal weakness, especially for males.

Crying children can make adults feel helpless. Out of a wish to protect children (and themselves), well-meaning adults often directly inhibit tears.

> **We, as caring adults, can acknowledge the sadness a child feels if he or she fails a test, repeats a school year, or strikes out in a baseball game.**
>
> **We, as caring adults, can acknowledge the sadness if the class is doing a Father's Day project and a child's dad is in the hospital, out of work, out of town, in jail, or has died.**
>
> **The child learns it is OK to feel his feelings.**

MYTH: AN ACTIVE PLAYING CHILD IS NOT A GRIEVING CHILD.

Don't expect children to mourn in the same way you do. Some may cry or say they are sad, some may appear not to be feeling anything, and others may show anger and hurt. All of these reactions need to be accepted.

Remember, a child can work out feelings best through play. What may appear to be a frivolous play activity to us may well be an important part of the mourning process.

Allison's best friend had moved away. She was missing her. A sensitive teacher gave her a toy telephone and suggested she call her. Allison began calling her on the play phone at school, telling her how much she missed her and asking when was she coming back? She was given an opportunity through play to work out her feelings.

MYTH: INFANTS AND TODDLERS ARE TOO YOUNG TO GRIEVE.

A dad told his boss at work, after the death of his oldest son, that he wouldn't explain anything to his two-year-old daughter because she was too young to understand.

Alan Wolfelt, noted clinical thanatologist and Director of the Center for Loss and Life Transition, emphasized that, "Any child who is old enough to love is old enough to mourn." *(Helping Children Cope with Grief,* 1983). Certainly toddlers and infants are capable of giving and receiving love—yet we often hear they are too young to understand.

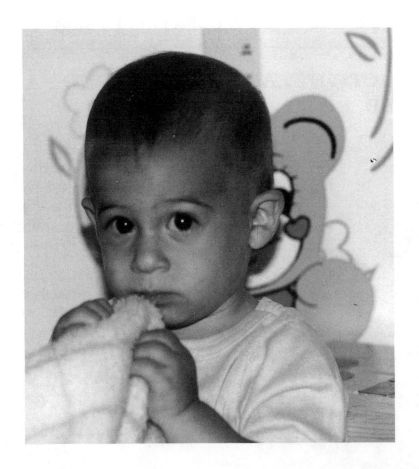

Ernie was dying. Diagnosed with a terminal pulmonary disease, he and his young wife bravely and determinedly decided to have a child—and to live to see him or her be born. With love and conviction, they accomplished their goal. Their son Eli was the joy of each of the precious days Ernie had left on earth. When Eli was two and a half months old, his dad died. A light went out in Eli's new life.

Fourteen months later, Eli and his mom were taking a walk and both spotted a man who remarkably resembled Eli's dad. Racing to the stranger, Eli wrapped his arms and legs around the man, clung to him with every ounce of Eli's little being, and refused to let go. His mom had to drag him away, sobbing.

At 16 months, Eli was mourning the death and the memories of his dad. Becoming noticeably sad after this experience, Eli began having difficulty with sleeping and eating. His mom decided to be open with him in talking and sharing feelings. Intuitively she knew a toddler was old enough to mourn, for he *certainly* had been old enough to love. She invited him to help create a photo album of Dad and times shared together.

This album became one of the great treasures of Eli's childhood. He carried his book of photos with him constantly, literally holding his dad's love in his arms. A tangible bridge of memories had been created between Eli and his Dad— a bridge of memories to last a life-time.

MYTH: PARENTS, EDUCATORS, AND CLERGY ALWAYS ARE PREPARED AND QUALIFIED TO GIVE EXPLANATIONS AND CLARIFICATIONS REGARDING LOSS AND GRIEF.

No one has all the answers, not even parents, teachers, counselors, or clergy. When our baby Jennifer died, my husband and I knew no guidelines to help us through such a tragedy. We turned to a rabbi for help. "Do we have a funeral?" "How do we bury her?" "What can we do for her?" "Don't worry," he said. "In the Jewish religion, stillborn babies are not considered a life." We had just seen her, held her, and gone through two days of labor and nine months of pregnancy with her. We knew she was a life. We sought council within ourselves and found the right answers for us.

I sat across the table from a pastoral counselor at a meeting on how to talk to children about death. The counselor was worried about a mother who insisted she had four children although one had died. The counselor wondered how she could help the mother see that she was going too far with her response by insisting she had four children. From the counselor's point of view, the mother clearly had three. The counselor felt that this mother's child was dead and that the mother needed to cope with reality. **But whose reality?—The mother's or the counselor's?** Clearly this rabbi and this pastoral counselor never had a child die. They would know, "Once a mom, always a mom" through all time and space.

Yet Susan Trout, Director for the Institute for Attitudinal Healing and author of *To See Differently* (1990), gave me a very precious gift by referring to Jennifer as "your daughter." It was the first time that any one had acknowledged verbally that I indeed had had a real daughter who died. Children need this validation, too, if a sibling dies, whether it be a preschooler, toddler, stillborn, or miscarriage. By referring to this death as "your sister" or "your brother," the child can become more easily in touch with all the powerful feelings that those words evoke.

MYTH: THE GOAL OF HELPING BEREAVED CHILDREN IS TO "GET THEM OVER GRIEF AND MOURNING."

Children and adults often are told that they "should be over it by now—It's been almost a year." Adults who believe this myth deny children the patience to live with and to work with their grief.

Danny's teacher responded to the death of Danny's mom by telling him, "You have to forget about this and go on." Danny said he felt like killing his teacher! The last thing Danny wanted to do was to forget his mom. He needed to remember her in a positive way to take her with him on his journey.

Jonathan woke up one morning and decided to bring in a picture of his pet cat, Susie, for show-and-tell. She had died a year ago. When he came home from school that day he asked if he could see where she was buried. This was a healthy request, moving him towards healing. Both examples illustrate that coping with loss is ongoing.

Adults and kids often equate getting over grief with forgetting the person, without realizing that their pain is what connects them to their loss. We need to find alternative ways that connect them to the lost person or event, diffuse the pain, and transform it into a positive experience.

MYTH: CHILDREN ARE BETTER OFF IF THEY DON'T ATTEND FUNERALS.

Not allowing children to attend funerals creates an environment of denial that does not allow them to participate actively in the grieving process. The funeral provides a structure for the child to see how people comfort each other openly, mourn a loved one, and honor his or her life. Children learn the ways we say good-bye to the remains of the person who died and how we show respect for the deceased.

Chad's dad Ray drowned at age 31. Chad was 7. Chad's grandfather told Chad of his dad's death, and they cried together for a very long time. Ray's body was found after several days of being in the water, necessitating a closed casket funeral.

The family, including Chad, worked together to select meaningful items to be placed in the casket. A picture of Chad, a letter from Ray's mom, and some other items were chosen. Chad was made an important part of the funeral process, and by being so, the funeral process became an important part of him.

During the ceremony, Chad leaned over to his grandfather and whispered, "Granddad, I'm using my imagination right now and pretending I'm reaching inside the coffin and hugging Dad." He needed to say good-bye and created a way to do so.

Children assuredly follow their hearts to find their own unique ways to work through grief. Being present at the funeral, placing personal mementos in the coffin, and participating in the ceremony are very concrete ways children can contribute to the process of saying good-bye.

My son Jonathan, age six, attended his first funeral when my sister's mother-in-law died. Jonathan said he wanted to go to the funeral, and he did. When the family was viewing the body, he wanted to look too. A slight panic ran through me as all of my training and knowledge said "yes," while I heard my mother's voice say, "no, go sit in the other room, Jonathan." The funeral director walked over to me and quietly said, "I didn't want to interfere, but I feel kids imagine far more and far worse if they aren't allowed to look at the body. " Gratefully, I agreed. Jonathan walked over, viewed the body, and was quite satisfied. Surprisingly, my mother easily adjusted to the change of circumstance. Relaying the story to a friend, I was told that her son had chosen not to see the body of his grandmother and continually asks questions like, "Was Grandma's body bleeding or bruised or broken?"

We often shield children from the funeral experience because we think it is too difficult. It is difficult. By being allowed to choose to participate in a funeral of someone to whom he was not deeply emotionally attached, Jonathan was freer to incorporate the event and become prepared for future funerals of more closely connected loved ones. He came to see death as an open part of life.

These myths are barriers to the grieving process. They disguise our own vulnerability and feelings of helplessness, and perpetuate a world of denial.

We need a new way of looking at a universal issue of grief. We need to educate ourselves and our communities to distinguish between fact and fiction so that our children can too.

Chapter 3

FOUR PSYCHOLOGICAL TASKS

OF

GRIEF WORK

UNDERSTANDING

GRIEVING

COMMEMORATING

GOING ON

"THERE ARE TWO CHOICES WHEN A LOVED ONE DIES—TO LIVE IN GRIEF, REMORSE, AND GUILT COVERED THINLY BY A FACADE; OR TO FACE THOSE FEELINGS, WORK THEM THROUGH, AND EMERGE WITH AN ACCEPTANCE OF DEATH AND A COMMITMENT TO LIVING."

Edith Mize, R.N.
in Elisabeth Kubler-Ross'
Death: The Final Stage of Growth (1975)

CHILDREN WORK THROUGH GRIEF: FOUR PSYCHOLOGICAL TASKS

Sandra Fox, past director of the Boston "Good Grief" program, listed four tasks children need to work through in order to grow. These tasks occur at every age level and in every type of loss. The four tasks are

UNDERSTANDING

GRIEVING

COMMEMORATING

GOING ON

UNDERSTANDING

Understanding is the first psychological task. Children need to make sense out of death. We need to define death as when the body stops working. Then each family can explain death in it's own way. Dr. Fox suggested this possibility: "In our family, we believe that when a person's body stops working he dies, but we believe his soul or spirit lives on in heaven with God" or "but we believe he lives on in some form of plant or animal life."

We can explain unexpected deaths by reminding kids that "Most people live to be very, very old, but once in a while a very bad accident, illness, or injury is so bad that doctors and hospitals can't help, and a person's body stops working."

We need to remember that children's understanding of death changes as they develop. Let's remember that kids perceive death differently at various childhood stages and that their perception is a predictable influence on grief.

UNDERSTANDING AFFECTED BY MAGICAL THINKING

Magical thinking is a predictable interference with children's grief. Children feel responsible for what happens in the world around them. When a six-year-old screams at her brother, "I hate you! I wish you were dead!" and these become the last words spoken to her brother who died in a drowning accident the following morning, magical thinking assuredly can make her feel she caused this death. She may live with overwhelming guilt for many years to come.

Five-year-old Sam announced he had "killed [his] Mother." His mother died of cancer. Yet, Sam had always heard that "junk food could kill you," and he had given her soda the day before she died. The family did not talk to him about cancer, believing it was too terrible to talk about. As an adult, Sam still believes at some deep emotional level that he is in someway responsible for killing his mother.

The movie "Home Alone" is a wonderful fantasy illustrating how powerful children's magical thinking is. The boy in the film was angry and frustrated with his family and went to bed wishing they would all disappear. He woke up in an empty house and was sure he had orchestrated their disappearance, even though they really had forgotten to take him on the family vacation.

UNDERSTANDING BLOCKED BY COMMON CLICHES

Common cliches can hurt the grief process. Mandy's grandfather died. Her mom thinks, "I'll just tell her he's gone to heaven and that will take care of it." Mandy wonders, "If grandpa is in heaven, why did they put him in the ground?" or "Can I go to heaven too?"

We need to give honest answers to questions about death, using simple and direct language. Facts need to be presented accurately. Children will find them out in time. **Telling children the truth will create an atmosphere of trust and confidence.** But children often take and believe what we say literally.

ALBERT LOST HIS MOTHER
-"He did! Where? How? Did he look for her? How could he lose her? She was so tall!" replied a panicked little voice.

-Children may fear the literal loss of their own parents.

-**It is better to say**, "Albert's mother died. He will miss her a lot."

DAD WENT ON A LONG TRIP
-"Why didn't he say good-bye? Where did he go?" his little daughter asked.

-Children may become afraid of anyone or themselves going on a trip. They may fear their parents leaving for work or generalize to just feeling abandoned.

-**It is better to say**, "Dad died in a drowning accident. We all feel so sad, but we will get through it together."

IT IS GOD'S WILL
(or "God took him because he is so good" or "He's in heaven with the angels.")
-"Why doesn't God take me? I'm good" or "I'll have to be bad so that God won't take me," thinks a little boy.

-A child may develop a fear of God or a fear of love.

-**It is better to say**, "Grandpa died last night. We will think about him a lot. We can remember all of the wonderful things we did with him."

GRANDMA IS WATCHING YOU IN HEAVEN
(so you better be good)

-The child thinks, "What happens if I'm bad?"

-Children can have paranoid feelings, become afraid of making mistakes, and feel guilty and stuck in any "bad" behaviors.

-**It is better to say,** "Grandma was very, very old and died. Her love for us will live on in our memories."

MAX (the cat) WENT TO SLEEP LAST NIGHT
(He's in kitty heaven)

-"Will I die when I go to sleep tonight?" the child wonders.

-Children may develop a fear of sleep or darkness that could result in sleeplessness and nightmares.

-**It is better to say,** "Max was very, very sick and the sickness made him die. No one really knows if he went to heaven. Some people believe that he does, and some people don't."

UNDERSTANDING CHILDREN'S DEVELOPMENTAL STAGES

A child's understanding of death changes as he or she develops. To know how children perceive death at different developmental stages of childhood is important so that we then can work with predictable and appropriate responses.

AGE 0-2
PIAGET'S STAGE OF DEVELOPMENT: SENSORIMOTOR

CHILD'S CONCEPT OF DEATH: "ALL GONE"

-"Out of sight, out of mind" appears to be the infant's perception. If the young infant cannot see something, it does not exist.

-Peekaboo or hide-and-seek are games that after six months help develop the concept that things and people exist even if we can't see them.

AGE 2-7
PIAGET'S STAGE OF DEVELOPMENT: PREOPERATIONAL

CHILD'S CONCEPT OF DEATH: MAGICAL, EGOCENTRIC, AND CAUSAL

-Child thinks death is temporary and partial.

-Preschoolers see death as reversible, a journey from which there is a return.

-A child conceives the possibility of reviving the dead person by giving hot food or keeping the body warm.
The child believes some functions continue like feeling and thinking.

-Children may see dead people as living in a box underground, connected to other boxes by tunnels, or on a cloud in a place called heaven. Jonathan, a six-year-old, explained that "Heaven is a place way deep underground, deeper than anyone has ever gone, deeper than bulldozers go. Your body disintegrates and goes there."

-The child thinks his or her own thoughts or actions could cause death. The child feels guilt and fear of retribution for perceived "bad things done or angry thoughts." A child tells Mom she hates her and wishes she was dead. Mom is killed in an accident the next day. The child's magical thinking convinces the child that she caused her mother's death.

-The child thinks death is like sleep. This creates a fear of sleep and darkness, and the child needs to be reassured.

-The child gives inaccurate estimates of an average life span. The child thinks that "people live for 150 years."

AGE 7-12
PIAGET'S STAGE OF DEVELOPMENT: CONCRETE OPERATIONS

CHILD'S CONCEPT OF DEATH: CURIOUS AND REALISTIC

-Children are curious and inquisitive about birth, death, and sex differences . They are very interested in details of death.

-Children begin to internalize the universality and permanence of death. They can conceptualize that all body functions stop.

-Dead people can't breathe, move, hear, or see. Children are aware of a death vocabulary. They can express logical thoughts and fears about death.

-Children can comprehend thoughts of a belief in an afterlife.

-Children can estimate accurately how long people live.

-Children think of death's occurrence in specific observable concrete terms. They may ask, "What are the reasons people die?" (War, poison, floods, car accidents, plane crashes, murders, etc.)

-Children basically still believe that the very old, the severely handicapped, and the extremely awkward people are the ones who die.

AGE 13 AND UP
PIAGET'S STAGE OF DEVELOPMENT: FORMAL OPERATIONS, IMPLICATIONS, AND LOGIC

ADOLESCENT'S CONCEPT OF DEATH: SELF-ABSORBED

-Adolescents understand mortality and death as a natural process.

-They often have a difficult time with death because they are absorbed with shaping their own lives. Death seems remote and something they can't control.

-The denial of their own death is strong. Adolescents usually feel death is caused by old age or serious illness.

-Adolescents are more comfortable talking about death with peers than with adults.

Julie and Lila are two young girls who chose to use writing as a way to work out their feelings. Julie, a five-year-old, had a cousin Mary who had died. Julie kept dictating letters to her cousin and asking Mother to mail them. Julie didn't understand that death was not reversible.

Ten-year-old Lila, mourning her Uncle Brian's death, had a different issue. Rather that writing to Brian, she wrote about Brian in private poetry she kept hidden in her room. She understood only too well how final death was but felt ashamed to share it.

At age five, Julie had no problem being open about her feelings, but she didn't really understand the nature of death. By age ten, Lila did understand what death was about, but she was uncomfortable being open about her feelings.

Uncle Bryan
is a
Flower Blooming

When he comes light-jogging
   into my arms...he delights me.
Like a child getting his own pet,
   And I still love him.
He always was playing sports
   And he puts a smile on my face.

When he comes light-walking
   into my heart
He opens his arms to me
Like vines wrapping around a tree
   ... and I love him.

Even though he is gone
Uncle Bryan is a flower
   blooming
   ... that fills me with joy.

by Lila Feikin (3/92)

Printed with permission.

GRIEVING

Grieving is the second psychological task for bereaved children and adolescents. Anger as well as grief must be dealt with, and many times anger is less acceptable to parents, schools, and communities. Children's grief is an ongoing process, often continuing through adolescence.

"WHEN SOMEONE YOU LOVE DIES, YOU HAVE A FEELING OF NUMBNESS; A YEARNING; AND A PROTEST. YOU HAVE LOST PART OF YOURSELF; YOU FEEL DISORGANIZED; AND YOU DO MUCH CRYING. YOU'RE RESTLESS, AND YOU MAY FEEL GUILTY. PERHAPS YOU COULD HAVE HELPED THE ONE WHO DIED BUT YOU DID NOT KNOW HOW. YOU ARE ANGRY BECAUSE THE PERSON DIED, AND YOU ARE ANGRY AT THE WORLD. YOU FEEL SO ALONE, AND LONELINESS IS ONE OF THE BIGGEST PROBLEMS OF GRIEF."

Edith Mize, R.N.
In Elisabeth Kubler-Ross' *Death: The Final Stage of Growth*

PHASES OF GRIEF

Phases of grief can resurface at any time. A number of grief educators have suggested that grief can be seen as occurring in four phases. They are

---

SHOCK AND DISBELIEF

SEARCHING AND YEARNING

DISORGANIZATION AND DESPAIR

REBUILDING AND HEALING

(Source: Carol and David Eberling, *When Grief Comes to School*, 1991.)

They are not rigid stages, but interchangeable and continuous processes.

We can see how they change through Bobby's story. Bobby's brother died when Bobby was eight years old. His **shock and disbelief** began. He was very confused. He couldn't understand how his brother could be in the hospital, in the ground, in the funeral home, in heaven, and living in Bobby's memory all within the same week. He **searched for meaning** in a world that made no sense. Years later, at age 12, he began acting out at middle school, creating concern in his teachers and parents. It turned out that he had been looking back on his brother's death with **despair,** believing his parents had let his brother die and would probably let Bobby die too.

A new phase of grief work had begun—**rebuilding and healing**. Bobby was reassured that everything had been done for his brother and would be done for Bobby if needed. He discovered he had done much for his brother by holding him and sharing toys. Bobby's giving had really made a difference that no one could take away.

Bobby had learned to feel pain, be out of control, and gain mastery over his feelings. He began using a punching bag to work out some of his anger and choosing times to be alone when he was frustrated. Bobby's family had communicated clearly when his brother died, yet still misconceptions arose at a different stage of grief.

WE CANNOT EXPECT TO EXPLAIN THE LOSS INSTANTLY, AND A CHILD CANNOT LEARN IT INSTANTLY.

The grieving process is ongoing and ever changing. As caring adults, we need to create an understanding of the grieving child for parents, teachers, counselors, and other school personnel.

SYMPTOMS OF NORMAL GRIEF

BEHAVIOR SYMPTOMS

sleeplessness	sighing	verbal attacks
loss of appetite	listlessness	fighting
poor grades	absent mindedness	extreme quietness
crying	clinging	bed-wetting
nightmares	overactivity	excessive touching
dreams of deceased	social withdrawal	excessive hugging

THOUGHT PATTERNS

inability to concentrate	preoccupation
difficulty making a decision	confusion
self-destructive thoughts	disbelief
low self-image	

FEELINGS

anger	depression	fear	intense feelings
guilt	hysteria	loneliness	feeling unreal
sadness	relief	anxiety	
mood swings	helplessness	rage	

PHYSICAL SYMPTOMS

headaches	pounding heart	empty feeling in body
fatigue	hot or cold flashes	tightness in chest
shortness of breath	heaviness of body	muscle weakness
dry mouth	sensitive skin	tightness in throat
dizziness	increased illness	stomachaches

COMMON FEELINGS, THOUGHTS, AND BEHAVIORS OF THE GRIEVING CHILD

Child *retells events* of the deceased's death and funeral.

Child *dreams* of the deceased.

Child *feels the deceased is with him or her* in some way.

Child *rejects old friends and seeks new friends* who have experienced a similar loss.

Child *wants to call home* during the school day.

Child *can't concentrate* on homework or class work.

Child *bursts into tears* in the middle of class.

Child *seeks medical information* on death of deceased.

Child *worries excessively* about his or her own health.

Child sometimes *appears to be unfeeling* about loss.

Child *becomes the "class clown"* to get attention.

Child *is overly concerned* with caretaking needs.

COMMEMORATING

The third task of grief is commemoration. Children need to establish ways to remember the person or animal that died or the object that was lost or destroyed. Involve kids in formal and informal ways to commemorate. Their creative ideas are an essential part of this process.

FORMAL COMMEMORATION

Schools, camps, and community groups can arrange memorial services, commemorative plaques, or tributes in a yearbook.
Scholarship funds, donations to a particular charity, or a memorial garden can be established.

INFORMAL COMMEMORATION

Children can bring seeds to plant flowers honoring a principal who died.
Children can choose a baseball book for the library to honor a child who loved baseball and was killed in an auto accident.
Children can create a school play and use the proceeds to begin a memorial fund in memory of a beloved teacher.
A class can decide what to do with the things inside the locker or desk of a boy who has died of cancer. They can make a booklet of memories for his parents.

Sandra Fox, author of *Good Grief: Helping Groups of Children When a Friend Dies* (1988), emphasized that **"The life of every person who dies needs to be commemorated if we are to teach young people that all lives have value."** Many schools are afraid to acknowledge a suicide, thinking denial may prevent further occurrences. By remembering a "too tragically short life" rather than the way someone died, the school can create a "teachable moment" to talk to kids about how to recognize and work through feelings of pain and hopelessness.

GOING ON

The last psychological task for children experiencing significant loss is one that emphasizes going on with fun activities. Kids can begin to risk loving again and enjoying life. This does not mean forgetting the person who's gone or the object (i.e., a toy or a pet). Going on means developing a readiness to participate. Sometimes it signals a release of some of the deep guilt that often is felt.

Ann's dad had been dead for two years. She finally thought, **"I don't need to visit Dad's grave so much. I can remember him in my mind a lot."** She now feels ready to go to the park where she spent so much time with Dad or let her Uncle Michael take her for ice cream the way Dad did.

Henry, whose best friend died in a car accident, tells his mom, **"I want to go out with my friends again. We were talking about how much fun we had with Bill when he was alive, and we decided to go swimming where we used to go with him."** The boys spent the day at the pool, reminiscing about old times with their friend.

Understanding, grieving, commemorating, and going on are important parts of the child's process of loss, change, and growth. Recognizing these tasks can create a richer picture of where the child is in his or her process. Caring adults can see if a child is stuck in one particular task and help him or her to work with the grief.

THE STORY OF STAR

Star was Tom's pet dog. Star was hit by a car and severely injured with no chance of recovery while Tom, a second grader, was at school. Tom came home and his dog was gone. He needed to **understand** why. His mom tells him, "Star was put to sleep." Tom imagines Star will wake up soon and be back. Mom says, "No, he's gone forever." Tom begins to worry that if he goes to sleep he too might not come back.

It's OK for him to see his mom crying because she saw Star's favorite ball. She loved him too. Kids need explanations of what is happening so that the missing pieces won't be filled in with their own unrealistic imagination and interpretation.

Give young children the simplest information possible while still sharing needed facts for their growth. "How did Star die? What did the vet do? Who took him to the vet? Did he cry? Where was he buried? Can I see?" All of these questions need to be answered. Finally we need to say, "Star won't be back. We won't see him again. His body has stopped working. It is very sad and we will miss him very much. We can give Star a funeral and say goodbye to him."

Tommy needs to work through the various feelings associated with **grieving.** He needs to

1. understand that the loss is real,
2. feel the hurt,
3. learn to live life without the lost object, and
4. transform the emotional energy of grief into life again.

Let Kids Know: "Star won't be in your daily life, but he will be in your memory."

Let Kids Talk: "I'm sad, angry, or frightened about what happened to Star. I feel so lonely without him."

Let Kids Participate: Tom can choose what to do with Star's toys, his bowl, or his collar. Where should we put his pictures? What kind of a ceremony would he like to have? Who would he like to invite?

Let Kids Be Unique: Each child is different and so is his or her grief. Tommy wants to build a doghouse where Star is buried. It's Tommy's own way of remembering Star.

Tom can **commemorate** Star's death informally or with a real ceremony. As long as Tom is involved, if he wants to be, he will be able to work through his grief. In this way he can affirm the value of the life that was Star's. Tommy decided to invite his family, neighborhood friends, and two pet dogs in the neighborhood. He read a poem, played music, and planted flowers as a tribute. He put a picture of Star by his bed to help remember him.

When Tommy has understood, grieved, and commemorated his dog's death, he is ready to **"go on."** This readiness involves knowing it's OK to start life again—to play with other dogs or even hope to get a new one. It's not the same thing as "forgetting." Star will live in Tommy's heart. It may hurt on Star's birthday or the day that he died, yet Tommy's grief experience with Star will strengthen Tommy's ability to cope with other losses that he assuredly will have as life goes on.

Chapter 4

TECHNIQUES FOR GRIEF WORK

IDENTIFY FEELINGS   STORY-TELLING

PUPPETS   ART   MUSIC   CLAY   SAND TABLE

DRAMA   ROLE-PLAYING   JOURNALS

MEMORY BOOKS

IDENTIFY FEELINGS

Children under stress tend to cut themselves off in the now, becoming often only half here. As caring adults, we can draw upon many techniques that will enable children to become more in touch with all aspects of themselves, and will enable them to communicate directly with others by being fully and completely present.

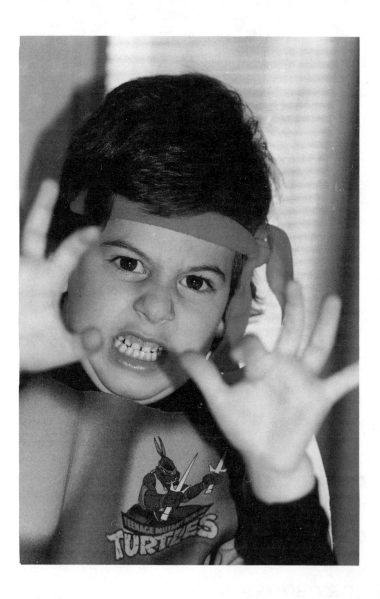

ANGER

"HOW COULD DADDY HAVE DIED AND LEFT ME ALL ALONE?"

Children feel angry about the death or illness of a loved one. Losses such as divorce, moving, or pet death certainly provoke anger. Feeling they have no control over what has happened, kids may project their angry feelings onto the person or thing that's gone, or doctors, teachers, parents, siblings, or God.

Kids learn at a young age not to express anger. They push it inward in order to get their needs met and to avoid being rejected or abandoned. Violet Oaklander, gestalt therapist and author of *Windows to Our Children* (1969), stressed that **"anger is an expression of self."**

If a child holds back and holds in, he gives his personal power away by projecting his real feelings onto another person or object. Sammy had been fighting on the playground a lot. His teacher asked, "Why?" "All the kids are mean," Sammy replied. Sammy's underlying anger was a dad who had abandoned him. He kicked and hit the kids on the playground instead.

Adults can help kids by **acknowledging** their angry feelings and guiding them to say, "I'm angry." Let them know it's OK to feel anger and own it as theirs. "It's OK that I'm angry."

We can build an **anger awareness** by talking with children.

What is anger? How does your body feel?

What could make you angry? How do you show anger?

What do you do when your angry?

Children then can use new skills to incorporate their anger. One productive expression of anger is direct communication, talking to the person with whom you are angry and telling him or her why you are angry. Another way to express anger personally is by taking the angry energy when it can't be expressed directly and using it in good ways.

Kids can take their anger and work with it in appropriate ways. They can vent angry energy by punching a pillow, building a project, using physical activity, role-playing, drawing or writing, or talking to a friend or adult.

I won't go to Grandma's. You could die while I'm away...like Daddy did!

PANIC

"MOMMY, ARE YOU GOING TO DIE TOO?"

Young children may have a huge fear of abandonment if one parent dies or leaves the house. They are afraid that if one parent has gone, the other could go too. They may cling to the remaining parent, refusing to play with friends or do other activities. Children need to rebuild trust. It takes time.

DENIAL

"I CAN'T BELIEVE GRANDPA DIED. HE COULDN'T HAVE DIED. HE'LL BE BACK."

Death, illness, or other loss comes as a surprise, and children as well as adults are shocked. If these experiences are overwhelming, kids may push them away as temporary relief from grief. Respect this as the child's way of saying what he or she can handle.

GUILT

Mom frowns. Ben thinks. **"I must have done something wrong to make her so angry. It's my fault. I've been such a bad kid lately!"** He didn't understand Mom had just heard bad news on the telephone. Children can't separate themselves from the experience. They take in an adult message, "swallow it," and "stuff it," sometimes carrying it all of their lives. Many of us live with the belief system of a four-year-old. We carry traumatic messages from early childhood, not only as if they were true then, but as if they are still true today.

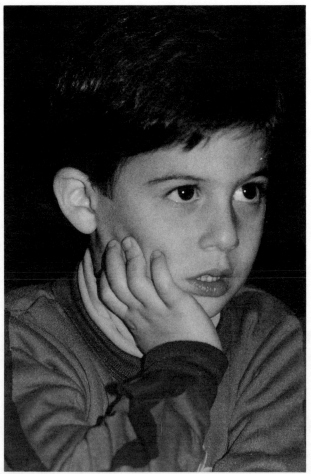

WITHDRAWAL

"I WON'T GO WITH THE NEW GYM TEACHER. I WANT TO BE ALONE"

Jason's mom's new boyfriend decided to stop being with Jason and his mom. Two years earlier Jason's dad had left town. Afraid to be vulnerable again, Jason withdrew from any new men who entered his life. The new gym teacher at school is a man. Jason refuses to go with the teacher and is sent to the principal's office for disobedience. No one understands that previous abandonment may have recreated Jason's fear of being hurt. Children may withdraw from loved ones as well as a safeguard against them leaving too. If kids have been traumatized too severely, they may be afraid to trust. Adults need to find creative ways to connect with children and build a relationship.

STUFFING THE FEELING

ADULTS OFTEN URGE CHILDREN TO STUFF OR DENY THEIR FEELINGS BECAUSE ADULTS ARE UNCOMFORTABLE WITH SEEING THOSE FEELINGS IN KIDS. "WHAT WE RESIST, PERSISTS!" THE MORE WE PROMOTE DENIAL OF FEELINGS, THE GREATER THE FEELINGS BECOME.

IDENTIFYING THE FEELING

WHEN CHILDREN'S FEELINGS ARE IDENTIFIED AND GIVEN A NAME, THOSE FEELINGS THEN ARE VALIDATED. ALTHOUGH ADULTS SOMETIMES FEAR NAMING FEELINGS WILL CREATE A LARGER PROBLEM, IT ACTUALLY REDUCES THE HURT BY BRINGING IT OUT INTO THE OPEN.

GRIEF RESOLUTION TECHNIQUES: IDEAS FOR ALL AGES

Techniques of grief resolution create and stimulate open discussion and exploration of feeling.

STORY-TELLING

Begin a story as "*I wish*" or "*If only*" or "*Once upon a time there was a_____ who died*" (got divorced, got sick, etc.). Each person in a small group continues the story.

Have children create this story. *Pretend you are an alien trying to find out what death is on earth* (Possible answers—final, stop breathing, mystery, universal, happens to everyone, out of our control).

CREATIVE WRITING

feeling journals   autobiographies   memory books

letters   essays

Letters to Loved Ones

Letters to loved ones are useful tools to work through held-in thoughts and feelings. Using specific headings such as "Dear Mom" or "Dear Uncle Tom" helps kids really project themselves into the letter. Be sure they understand the loved one is not really getting the letter, but they can have a choice in the decision of what they want to do with it.

Dr. Lori Weiner, Coordinator of Pediatric HIV Psychosocial Support Program, American Cancer Institute, generously donated the following letter and drawing. Her work with children and AIDS has led her to feel that "the most exquisite, intense, intimate, and painful life experiences have been those where we have been given the opportunity to give to another human being and the strength to let go and say good-bye" (*Social Work*, Sept. 1991, 375-8).

Sara's dad died of AIDS. Her mom is HIV infected and so is Sara. Sara has two siblings. She is ten years old.

Dear Mom.

I miss you. Sometimes I get scared when you get sick. I worry that you will not come home. I want you to take care of yourself. If you ever got real sick will you tell us? I worry too much. I worry about you because you might get sick, not tell me and die. If you died I would be really upset and sad and cry a whole lot. I cried last night because I missed you so much. Sometimes I worry about me getting sick too and what you would do if I got real sick. Like would you cry or would you come see me in the hospital? If you were in the hospital I want to come see you.

Sometimes I even think about heaven. It is quiet and peaceful there and I know that you and I will be there together one day.

Mommy I love you and know you love me.

Sara

ME and MOMMY in Heaven

Ashley's mom died, at age 29, of a sudden heart attack. Ashley was six years old.

Dear Mom,
I really miss you.
I am doing fine in school. I think about you every day. I am really sorry you had to go down there. I wouldn't like it there myself. I don't know yet what to give you for mother's day.

Love,
Ashly

Essays can be used as grief resolution techniques. Not only do these essays allow students to express their feelings, but teachers and college personnel can know and understand how profoundly these loss and grief experiences affected the lives of these kids and assuredly shape who they are.

Essays

The following essay was written by Alison Rothenberg, a seventeen-year-old junior in high school. She was asked to write as a college entrance requirement an important experience that greatly affected her life. She wrote the following warm and sensitive tribute to her dad, Alan, who died when she was seven.

Ten years ago, my father, Alan Lee Rothenberg, died. He was my best friend when I was seven years old. He became sick and had to go into the hospital. I asked my mom, "Is he going to die?" She said, "Of course not," and told me not to think like that again.

His death shocked me, and no one in my family expected something so tragic to happen. After all my dad died at the early age of thirty-nine. When my mother told my brother and me, we were stunned. My brother, Andy, was only four and didn't understand but knew something bad had happened. I thought it was a nightmare, I couldn't comprehend it. The thought of his death scared me. I didn't even know what to say, but when I realized it was true I cried my eyes out. I remember my mom and I cried so much that we went through a whole box of kleenex.

I kept my feelings inside me for a long time, but as I got older and began to understand "why" it became easier to express how I felt. I'm so grateful that we spent special moments together. Things like driving his car while I was sitting on his lap in an empty parking lot or trying on his shoes and acting like a clown. We'd always end up laughing and spending unforgettable times together.

I remember my dad told me to strive for the best, and if I really put my mind to it , my wishes would come true. Well, two birthdays had gone by and the only thing that I wished for on my candles was to have my dad come back. This was one of the only wishes that never came true and the most important.

I miss him a lot, but I know he's out there somewhere looking out for me and guiding me in the right direction. I still feel there is a part of him with me—after all, we both have the same middle name, and my family and friends always tell me and my brother how much we resemble my dad.

Thanks to my dad's saying, "Strive for the best," I never settle for anything but that. His words keep me moving. Even though he's gone, I always have the memories. Those will never die.

Eric Dreisen, a fifteen-year-old, wrote the following article in his school newspaper after his mom's death. He hoped to reach out to other teens who had also experienced the death of someone close to them.

Help With Tough Times

by Eric Dreisen '95

As some of you might be aware, my mother passed away from cancer this school year. In experiencing this loss, there have been some positive things that have come from it. i have learned to take care of myself, my family and friends have become more important, and I have learned to help other perople who are going through tough times.

The purpose of this article is to invite any student who is suffering from a loss or who is going throughj tough times, to meet on a regular basis as a group to talk about the problem. i will organize this group by having speakers come or get information to help with this long, hard process. Please contact me at _____

_____ .

Memory Books

Memory books are extremely useful tools to allow children to express feelings and complete unfinished business (what they didn't get a chance to say). Inside the memory book, kids can use stars, stickers, photographs, and other decorations. Kids can make many different kinds of pages. Here are a few suggestions.

THE MOST IMPORTANT THING I LEARNED FROM THE PERSON IS . . .

WRITE A LETTER.   DEAR _____, LOVE,_____

WHAT IS THE FUNNIEST MEMORY YOU HAVE?

MY MOST SPECIAL MEMORY IS. . .

IF YOU COULD TELL YOUR LOVED ONE JUST ONE MORE THING, WHAT WOULD YOU SAY? WHAT DO YOU THINK THEY WOULD TELL YOU?

The following are four memory book illustrations. They were donated by Allyson Nuggent, bereavement counselor at the Stella Marris Hospice in Baltimore, MD. The first picture was made by a thirteen-year-old boy after his father died of a heart attack. The boy illustrated his view of the funeral in great detail. The next picture shows a young girl's perception of life before and after her dad's suicide. A six-year-old girl explored her feelings about her dad's death in the last two pictures.

Family and Friends come to a funeral service to remember a special person and to show their love for you.

What did you see at the funeral?

The thing that worries me
the most since the death of
my person is....
becaues my family is sad.
This is a picture of what
I am worried about

R.I.P.

I Get Angry About
~~they DiD not do anything~~ to him
since the death of my Person

I show my Anger by
telling Someone

This is me when I Am
! Angry !

Melissa is a thirteen-year-old whose father died of lung cancer. Her love for him shines through her warm memory of her dad.

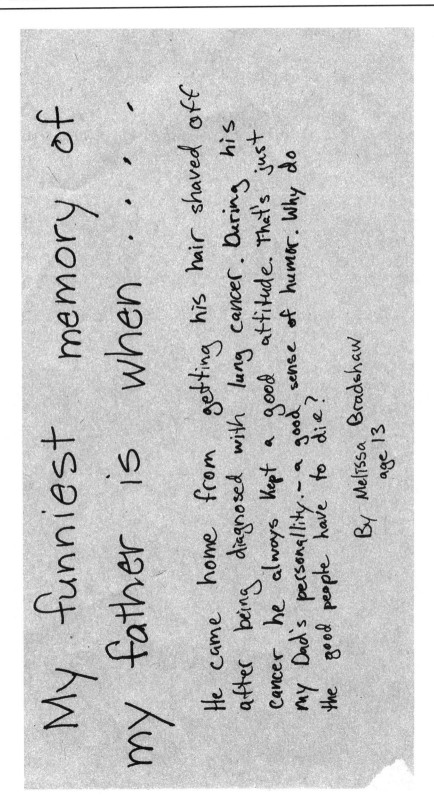

My funniest memory of my father is when . . .

He came home from getting his hair shaved off after being diagnosed with lung cancer. During his cancer he always kept a good attitude. That's just my Dad's personality.—a good sense of humor. Why do the good people have to die?

By Melissa Bradshaw
age 13

DRAMA AND IMAGINATION

Children use drama and imagination with props, costumes, and puppets to help them act out and identify feelings and thoughts. The young child can use the **toy telephone** to call someone who is gone. Kids can safely talk into a **tape recorder** to express unresolved feelings. **Puppets** are wonderful tools to create an imaginary dialogue between a child and someone who has left. **Dress up** for young children is another technique enabling them to immerse themselves in role-playing, becoming the loved one or another member of the family. Children also can role-play with **toy figures** or figures in a **sand table** to show how they feel.

FANTASY IS A POWERFUL TOOL FOR PROJECTION.

STIMULATING OPEN DISCUSSION

Polaroid pictures create good encouragement for open dialogue. By taking a polaroid picture of the child and placing it within one of his or her drawings, the child can project himself or herself into the drawing and begin to role-play. **Photographs** are a safe and natural way to communicate about the person who died. We sometimes can ask the children to help make **scrapbooks** about their loved one. This not only stimulates conversation but creates a memory to keep for years to come. **Personal items** specially chosen by the child that belonged to the deceased also are a wonderful remembrance and a way to keep getting to know what that person was like as the child gets older.

ART

The media of art also can promote open discussion and enhance open feelings. Children can

Draw the loss (death, divorce, moving, etc.).

Draw how they would like it to be.

Draw their house and who's inside.

Draw "What Makes Me Batty." Kids write feeling words as they talk about what bothers them.

Draw a mural as a group of the common loss.

Make a class booklet with words, pictures, poems, and photos.

Draw scribbles on a large piece of paper. Let the child choose a section, create a drawing, and talk about it. Give the drawing a title, and it becomes a story for discussion.

Children can choose from lots of art materials, such as size and color of paper, and what kind of crayons, pens, or markers they want to use. As children draw we can ask:

Do you mind if I watch you draw?
Can you tell me about your picture?

Begin a dialogue that will create a story. The parent, teacher, or counselor can come closer to the picture to see if there is something in it the child can identify with and ask, "Tell me more about it?". The child may realize then that the dog he or she drew in the picture is connected to him or her. "I'm like that dog. I bark at my sister all day."

> **Interpretation has limited value to children. Even if it's correct, it may not help the child express his or her feelings.**

Clay

Clay is a very versatile medium to use with children. It is reusable and an easy material with which to work. Kids can mold their family, friends, or animals and create dialogues between themselves and others. Clay has a very calming effect for children, and they can gain a feeling of mastery by working with it. Kids interact with clay by pounding it, squeezing it, pinching it, ripping it, smoothing it, and poking it. Lots of feelings can be expressed in a safe way.

Joey made a figure of his deceased brother out of clay. When asked, "What would you like to say to him?", Joey began to say good-bye. "You were a good brother, sorry you had to die." Then he kissed the figure. Joey also made the doctors that took care of his brother. "I hate you!" he shouted, "You wouldn't let me scream." He began pounding the clay and smashing it to bits. He certainly was using the clay as a good projective tool to express his anger.

Memory Boxes

Memory boxes are an excellent craft project for grieving children. Children can collect special articles that belonged to or reminded them of the person who died. These objects can be put in a shoe box and decorated by the child as a valuable treasure of memories. It also can serve as a tool for stimulating conversation.

MUSIC

Music can be used as a resource to explore feelings. Kids can listen to sounds that different instruments make to create feelings.

drums—anger   tuba—awkwardness
harmonica—loneliness   cymbals—shock
bells—sadness   harp—angel-like

Feelings can be projected into the music through body movement and dance. Doing so feels very freeing to children. Hap Palmer's album, "Feelings," is wonderful to use with young children.

RESOURCE LIBRARY

A resource shelf at home or in school is very important for kids. Be sure to include age appropriate children's literature on the grief and loss issue they are experiencing. Here are some useful suggestions:

The Creative Journal for Children by Lucia Capacchione (1982). A guide containing exercises in writing and drawing to promote self-esteem in children.

Put Your Mother on the Ceiling by Richard De Milleis (1973). Another good resource filled with children's imagination games.

Be a Bird, Be a Frog, Be a Tree by Rachel Carr (1973). A picture guide for using creative movement (yoga) with young children.

Changing Families (Fassler et al., 1988) and ***The Divorce Workbook*** (Ives et al., 1985) by David Fassler, Michele Lash, and Sally Ives. A wonderful interactive guide for kids and adults to work through feelings associated with divorce, separation, single family homes, moving, and step families.

When Someone Very Special Dies (1988), ***When Mom and Dad Separate*** (1990), and ***When Someone Has a Very Serious Illness*** (1991) is a series of workbooks by Marge Heegaard that allow the child to interact through drawing and writing to develop coping mechanisms and increase communication.

Kids can identify feelings by

1. Painting a picture of the feeling. "How does your anger look when your mom yells at you?"
2. Keeping an ongoing notebook of feelings with writing and drawing.
3. Doing feeling homework. Make a list of what makes you angry, sad, afraid, frustrated, etc.
4. Creating the feeling out of sand, clay, or puppets.

Parents can help kids identify feelings at home by

1. Allowing kids to identify and express dislikes openly. Make up a game with them saying what they don't like.
2. Having a Mad Session. During the routine bedtime ritual, parents can ask "Is there anything that made you mad today?" Be sure not to make any judgements or comments on answers.
3. Practicing yelling "no" or pounding on a pillow.
4. Reading books that open feelings discussion.
5. Talking about things. "What was your nightmare about last night? Let's see if you can draw what frightened you."

An important part of all of these techniques is that they have projective value. Children can't easily integrate their emotions and their intellect. Our job as caring adults is to help children reach all the parts of themselves that may have been cut off. We can do this by creating a relationship whereby two people can interact in an atmosphere that honors and respects who they are.

Chapter 5

PREPARING FOR A GOOD-BYE VISIT

YOU KNOW GRANDPA IS VERY SICK
HE'S GOING TO DIE SOON
HE PROBABLY WON'T TALK MUCH
HE LOOKS TERRIBLE

LET'S PREPARE KIDS TO SAY GOOD-BYE

Preparing a child for a "good-bye" visit to a dying loved one is a topic usually avoided or denied in our culture. A visit to an aging, sickly grandparent can be approached in a sensitive way.

To include children in the decision making is important. **Does the child want to visit the ill person?** If he or she answers "no," **find out what the fears are.** If discussed openly, these fears could be eliminated. **Talk about the hospital** and the room where the sick person will be. **Explain how he or she will look** and how his or her physical appearance may have changed with the illness. Suggest **bringing a gift** to the loved one. It's another way of saying good-bye. Make **visits brief** and provide space, both in time and location, for kids to discuss, write, or draw how they feel after their visit.

To prepare kids for the visit we need to be **honest in language and feelings**. Kids can and often do model themselves after the adults.

"Grandpa had a heart attack last night. He is very sick," Mom explains. Ben asked, "Will Grandpa die?" —a very common and direct question. "He may," his mom answered, adding hopefully, "but the doctors are working very hard to make him well again!" "I was scared when I heard about Grandpa, and very sad," Mom confided. "Is that how you feel? What can I do to help you?"

Because adults are often not sure what to say, it is necessary to provide comfortable language to use.

The following is a wonderful account of how a family approached their good-bye visit. "Preparing a Child for a Good-bye Visit to a Dying Loved One" is an article written by Judith Rubenstein, *JAMA*, May 14th, 1982 Vol. 247, pp. 2571-2572 (Copyright 1982, American Medical Association). It explains a farewell to a grandfather dying of cancer. The children, ages four and six, were prepared by the parents, and their mother tells the story.

THE SITUATION

There was no denying Grandpa was dying. My husband, who rarely travels, was suddenly making frequent short trips to Chicago to visit him. The children overheard the anxious, daily, long-distance telephone calls to or from my mother-in-law, and afterward the anxious conversations between my husband and me.

The children had a loving relationship with their Grandpa, built on pleasant visits several times a year when Grandma and Grandpa would come to Boston from Chicago. I remember in particular tireless sessions teaching toddlers to walk, and then later, long intimate walks, sometimes including "rest stops" at the candy or toy store.

Because of this warm relationship, we felt that the older children were entitled to say good-bye to him. . . . We decided that I would take our 6-year-old daughter to Chicago on one trip, and my husband would take our 4-year-old son on a separate trip.

Many people, friends, and family, strongly objected. They said, ... "Let them remember him the way he was." "He has deteriorated, and his changed appearance will frighten them." We rejected this well-meaning counsel in the belief that children have to learn that, however sad, sickness ending in death is part of life and that human beings have a need to say good-bye when time shared is over, whether it is a short, social visit or life itself.

OUR WORDS

My husband and I together spoke to each child alone. We chose the time after breakfast one morning, since our children were most refreshed and alert at that time of day. Also, they had the rest of the day to think and ask questions. (Speaking of such an emotional concept in the evening would only have upset bedtime.) Our presentation to each child took only five or ten minutes, including questions from the child and repetitions by us. We began something like this:

"We have something important to talk to you about. Come and sit on my lap. I'm going to Chicago in a few days to see Grandpa, and I'd like to take you with me, if you want to go. Before you decide, listen to what we have to say."

The children wanted to go. They responded to our statements as we made them, and my husband and I backtracked and repeated, and our presentation was not a smooth monologue, but we did speak the following phrases in more or less the following order:

You know Grandpa is very sick. He is going to die soon.

This probably will be the last time you will see him.

He's changed a lot since you saw him last.

He looks terrible.

He's very thin. He's very pale. He's very weak.

He probably won't talk much. He may cry.

But you don't have to be afraid.

He's still your same Grandpa.

He's unhappy because he knows he's going to be dying soon, and he
doesn't want to leave us.

You may give him a big hug and kiss.

It will make him feel better.

You don't have to be afraid to kiss him.

You can't catch his sickness. It's not a kind of sickness you can catch.

You love your Grandpa, and he loves you.

You may tell him you love him, if you want to.

That will make him feel good, too.

Following our explanation, each child asked more questions. Both children wanted to be reassured that they wouldn't catch any "germs" from Grandpa, and we repeated that his illness didn't have germs one could catch. Then the conversation turned to details of travel in the airplane, who else we would see in Chicago, and more questions about "germs." Then, before the questions and repetitions became too great, and the emotional tension turned to annoyance, we ended the conversation with:

We have talked enough for now. If you have any questions or if you want to talk about it again, you can ask us later. You can go play now.

Throughout that day and the following ones, the children asked questions from time to time while I was preparing a meal or folding laundry, or doing some quiet task not focused on the child, and we discussed the ideas again, but in a more casual way.

THE VISIT

A few days later, when my 6-year-old daughter and I visited my father-in-law, he was in pajamas in a wheelchair in the hospital waiting room. A compassionate physician and a humane hospital policy made this possible. My daughter approached him with poise, self-confidence and affection, without fear, lugubriousness, or false cheerfulness. She said, "Hi Grandpa." She reached up and put her arms around his neck and kissed his cheek. She smiled coyly and handed him a slip of paper on which she had drawn a picture and written, "I love you."

Grandpa and granddaughter hugged each other and smiled. The old man started to cry, and the little girl slipped down and sat on a chair. The adults talked a while longer, and then we left. As I pushed open the heavy glass doors to leave, my daughter turned and waved good-bye to Grandpa and followed me, skipping and smiling. The next week, my husband told me that he and our 4-year-old son had a similar experience at their visit.

In the years following my father-in-law's death, our children have mentioned that last visit from time to time. Although their remembrance of specific details, including their conversation, has blurred, they speak of the visit with a certain wistful pleasure, which makes us happy that we did not deny it to them.

From JAMA, May 14, 1982--Vol 247, No. 18. Reprinted with permission.

DO TALK WITH CHILDREN ABOUT DEATH

WAYS THAT WORK

Realize grief is an ongoing process with no easy answers.

Allow new loss to be the first priority with child's classmates.

Trust your instincts.

Initiate discussions of loss issues if child does not.

Encourage children to attend funeral if they choose.

Consider ways to commemorate loss (bulletin board display, letters to family, letters to person who died, photographs, memory book, tree planting).

Realize that not talking about the loss doesn't make it go away.

What we resist, persists!

Encourage classmates to be a support system.

Recognize laughter and play does not mean a child is not grieving.

Understand separation is the underlying pain of a grieving child.

Acknowledge children often believe they have magical powers and need to create a reason for what has happened.

COMMUNICATE WITH CHILDREN BY

Using children's own language

Realizing children can talk about their own experiences

Allowing children to ask their own questions

Creating honest discussion

Listening, watching, and waiting for the child to process his or her experience

Explaining to children the facts surrounding the loss

Chapter 6

ESPECIALLY FOR EDUCATORS:

THE BALL'S IN YOUR COURT

IDENTIFY CHILD   RECOGNIZE GRIEF AS A CRY FOR HELP

FIND RESOURCES   INSIST ON GETTING HELP

WE CAN MAKE A DIFFERENCE

Educators are frustrated, overwhelmed, and drowning in accountability. Too often they lack immediate resources to help them pull a child through a period of crisis.

While waiting to present a seminar on loss and grief issues to elementary school counselors, one counselor confided a very *unique* yet typical story.

Joey's mom had died when Joey was seven. He was in second grade. An Aunt reluctantly took him in. He began having severe attention-learning problems and acting out behaviors after his mom's death. (Wouldn't we all if our entire life was turned upside down in one week?) In first grade Joey had been a good student, achieving on grade level in reading and math. He was well liked by students and teachers. For the following two years he had no counseling or psychological help. His disruptive behaviors and ill performance in school were factors leading to his placement in a Level IV learning disabled class. The counselor sadly relayed the story. She felt defeated that a child had fallen through the cracks of the educational system. Left on this path, he very well may be headed for the penal system next.

LIFE IS A PROCESS: LOSS—CHANGE—GROWTH

"Two of the best kept secrets of the twentieth century are that everyone suffers and that suffering can be used for growth."
Lawrence LeShan (Jackson, 1973)

Life is a process of loss, change, and growth. Understanding loss issues can make them more predictable and therefore less frightening. Through grief we can grow in inner and outer strength and a healing can take place.

EDUCATORS FACE LOSS ISSUES DAILY

Educators face loss issues every day with their job, the kids with whom they work, and the system in which they work. They may ask themselves these questions:

Will I get a raise?

Will I get the promotion?

Will I get my materials?

Will I lose my job?

Will I be accountable to parents, children, and administrators when I walk through the door?

Will I get the respect I need in the classroom today?

Will I achieve my learning with the children?

Will I be a victim of violence in the school?

CHILDREN FACE LOSS ISSUES DAILY

Kids face loss issues every day with teachers, other kids, and the system. They may ask themselves these questions:

Will I lose the baseball game?

Will my best friend like someone else?

Will the kids pick on me at lunch?

Will I fail a test?

Will I fail this grade?

Will I forget my homework?

Will my teacher like me?

Will I learn today?

Will my sick mother be OK when I'm at school?

Will they think I'm different because I go to speech class?

Will they make fun of my braces, my skin, my hair, my sex?

Will anyone discover my secrets? (Mom got drunk last night. Dad came into my bedroom. My brother got arrested by the police.)

BOBBY AND GREGORY'S STORY:
A CHILD'S VOICE IS HEARD

While working as a counselor in a school where the majority of children came from divorced and single parent homes, I met Bobby, a bright sixth grader. He had flourished under the love and support of his foster parents during the two years he had lived with them. They adored Bobby and Bobby adored them. Bobby and I would play chess in my room, and he would speak fondly of his natural mother, but spoke of his foster mother as "Mom."

One day the courts decided that Bobby would be better off going back to his natural mom. **No one asked him how he felt**. Bobby moved back. The devastation of that act wreaked havoc on the emotional and physical well-being of both Bobby and his foster parents. Within a few months Bobby's grades dropped, his smile dimmed, and his natural mom began drinking again. **No one had asked Bobby how he felt, and no one had offered a solution.**

Many Bobbys have been and still are in the school system. One such Bobby, actually named Gregory, recently broke new ground by coming up with his own solution and making headlines in 1992.

Gregory contacted a lawyer on his own, and expressed his strong desire to terminate his parents parental rights and divorce them. This was the first time a child had sued his parents on his own right. Usually an adult, guardian, or friend sues on behalf of the child. Gregory felt his mom and dad had abandoned and neglected him. He wanted the courts to consider children's choices in domestic matters and have children be "treated as people and not as property."

Gregory had found a permanent, stable home and wanted to stay there. His voice **needs to be heard** as part of the legal requirements in our courts. Kids need protection for their rights to participate in divorce and foster care decisions in the judicial system when the parental and governmental systems have not worked for them.

WE CAN SEE THE DAY DIFFERENTLY

We as educators need to identify the behaviors, thoughts, and feelings that grief and loss issues bring to the foreground. Our school day is an ongoing kaleidoscope of children working through their many grief processes.

All children's "acting out" or "acting in" behaviors are their cries for help. These behaviors may be a red flag to adults that a child is working through a grief issue.

We can create a **SAFE** and feeling environment for kids by turning humiliations into an arena of self-esteem. So often these grief issues have an immediate and direct effect of lowering self-esteem and creating guilt and shame, the underlying force behind many of these behaviors.

Let's have the patience to wait before responding, and to think before we act so that we can:

S—Seize the moment. Guide the child to give a good answer, rather than condemn a bad one. The goal is not to learn the facts, but to love learning.

A—Act. When in doubt, reach out. It works. Kids feel sincerity. Children respond to warmth and caring.

F—Find strengths. Every child has them. Children are taught to stuff feelings, and these feelings come out in other ways. If we really knew what was pushing that child to act out, we would never judge them.

E—Establish a relationship. Talk to the child alone. Let the child know you are aware of his or her behaviors, and that you will be there if he or she needs to talk.

Children will be more open to learning and relating if they are given avenues to express their bottled up feelings. Their academic, social, and spiritual growth will soar with the release of stored up hurts.

TEACHABLE MOMENTS

"Teachable moments" is an important concept for **unplanned** lessons. A "teachable moment" is a spontaneous mini-lesson inserted into the daily planned activities based on something that has just happened. Its **power** comes from catching the moment and creating a living, dynamic learning situation.

"Teachable Moments" can be <u>trauma</u> related or a <u>natural</u> <u>part</u> of the day. It is important to seize these opportunities and not deny their value. Mrs. Albert, a kindergarten teacher, confided her feelings of fear and inadequacy that held her back from relating in the here and now. Karen, a five-year-old, had recently experienced the death of her dad. Every time she mentioned Daddy, Mrs. Albert ignored her. This went on for three months. The teacher explained that she didn't know what to say, and so she avoided any mention of Dad in the classroom.

Sometimes we can integrate special vocabulary to help ease the flow of conversation. Open-ended questions allow the child to remember and verbalize events and feelings. Mrs. Albert could have asked Karen, "What are some of the times you remember best with your Dad?", giving Karen an avenue for sharing. Had she asked a closed question such as, "Do you remember some good times with your Dad?", Karen could have easily just answered, "Yes."

Integrating a "teachable moment" into the classroom can be done easily if a class goldfish dies or if a dead worm is found after it rains. As educators, we can

**explain it is part of the life cycle,
have a funeral for it,
bury it,
talk about feelings,
make a class "memory book" or "memory box,"
and/or read the books *Lifetimes* (Mellonie & Ingpen, 1983) and *About Dying* (Stein, 1974).**

> **Hands-on practical curricula and manuals are available that provide lesson plans specific to each grade level.**

An example might be a first grade having a lesson involving the understanding of differences between dead and alive. Kids can examine alive and dead plants, which could lead them into a discussion of the concept that when we die our bodies stop working. These materials suggest readings such as *Lifetimes* (Mellonie & Ingpen, 1983) or *About Dying* (Stein, 1974) for young children.

In contrast, the fourth-grade lessons provide ideas to introduce discussion of loss and that it's OK to have your feelings. Suggested activities include speakers covering topics from losing a sports championship to a house being destroyed by a fire. Kids can brainstorm losses in groups and discuss them, collect newspaper articles on loss, or keep loss journals. *Charlotte's Web* (White, 1952) is a wonderful book to use with this age child. *The Hurt* by Teddi Doleski (1983) is a book for all ages that illustrates that the hurt grows when we hold onto it, and "magic" can happen when we let it go. Resource corners in each classroom and school library would benefit children of all ages.

A good example of integrating a trauma into a "teachable moment" was that of a caring fourth grade teacher. The children in her class were talking about nightmares and drawing pictures after hearing on the news about a seven-year-old who was attacked brutally by dogs. The class began writing the little girl and even collecting money for a Michael Jackson tape for her.

This teacher had chosen to transform the children's fear into a positive, empowering memory. Art Kirsch, educator and director of Detroit's "Kids In Crisis Program," emphasized that these "emotional inoculations" of teachable moments are literally a shot in the arm for preparing children for their own next loss. Hopefully, the more comfortable we as educators become with these grief and loss issues, the more we can become role models for children to work through their grief. Through education, we can become increasingly aware of our own barriers and can conquer and dispel the myths.

GUIDELINES FOR EDUCATIONAL REFERRAL

Become familiar with local agencies and their programs. They can provide help for children and their families to connect them with community resources.

1. Present observations and concerns honestly to both parents if possible. Be clear, organized, and specific. Use a children's loss inventory as a resource. (A sample Children's Loss Inventory Checklist has been provided in this book.)

2. Find out if the child is or was in counseling, and if the parents are familiar with specific community resources. (A sample list of community resources is provided in Chapter 7.)

3. Offer to share information and observations with a person in the community of the parents' choice.

4. Maintain the privacy of the child. Only talk about the child with resource personnel in other agencies with the parents' permission.

5. Obtain written authorization from a parent or guardian before releasing information. Protect the rights of the child and family. Date request and specify person in agency.

6. Suggest several possibilities for help to parents. Let them find the one that feels right to them.

7. Let parents schedule the referral appointment.

8. Suggest that the parents follow up with you after their first appointment.

9. Ask the parent to keep you informed of any ways you can help the child during this period.

10. Keep a list of significant dates (birth dates or date of loss) that may affect the child throughout school.

CHILDREN'S LOSS INVENTORY CHECKLIST:
A COMPLETE PICTURE OF THE WHOLE CHILD

IDENTIFY CHILD

Name_____Age_____Grade_____

Address_____Birthdate_____

Phone number_____Today's date_____

REFERRAL INFORMATION

Reasons for referral _____

_____

Source of referral_____

IDENTIFY RECENT SIGNIFICANT LOSS

Relationship of deceased to child_____

What are the facts about the loss? (Who or what, where,how)

_____

_____

Who told the child?_____

How was he/she told?_____

Date of birth of deceased_____Date of death of deceased_____

PREVIOUS LOSS AND GRIEF HISTORY

Include significant dates or birth dates involved in previous losses.

Divorce or Separation_____Date_____

Moving_____Date_____

Friends Move Away_____Date_____

Past Deaths_____Who?_____Date_____

Pet Deaths_____Who?_____Date_____

Parents Changing Job_____Date_____

Parents Losing Job_____Date_____

Fire_____Robbery_____Date_____

Other_____Date_____

INHERITED FAMILY LOSS

Examples are a grandfather killed in a war or a previous sibling death

_____.

FAMILY UNIT

Single Parent_____ Divorce_____

Unmarried_____ Adoption_____

Natural parents_____ Blended family_____

FAMILY HISTORY OF CHRONIC CULTURAL LOSS

Drugs_____ Injuries_____

Crime_____ Unemployment_____

MEDICAL HISTORY

Significant Parent Illness_____

Significant Children's Illness_____

PREVIOUS SCHOOL HISTORY

Grades_____

Progress_____

Participation_____

ASSESSMENT HISTORY

Standardized Tests_____Date_____

_____

Speech and Language Evaluation _____Date_____

_____

Educational Assessment_____Date_____

_____

Psychological Evaluation_____Date_____

_____

IDENTIFY CHILD'S ATTITUDE TOWARDS SIGNIFICANT OTHERS

Siblings_____

_____

Parents _____

_____

Friends_____

_____

Pets_____

_____

Self_____

_____

IDENTIFY LIKES AND DISLIKES

Interests_____

Likes_____

Dislikes_____

Abilities_____

Likes_____

Dislikes_____

IDENTIFY PRESENT BEHAVIORS AT SCHOOL

(Check those that apply)

Disruptive in school_____Failing grades_____

Inability to concentrate_____Increased absenteeism _____

Fighting with peers_____ Withdrawn_____

Using bad language_____Very tired_____

Physical complaints (headaches, stomachaches)_____

Nervous_____ Other_____

IDENTIFY PRESENT BEHAVIORS AT HOME

(Check those that apply)

Less interactions_____Sleeplessness_____

Poor eating_____ Bed-wetting_____

Clinging to parents_____ Nightmares_____

Increased perfectionism_____Crying_____

Excessive talk of loss_____

Fighting with siblings or parents_____

Fear of dark, noise, or robbers_____

IDENTIFY PRESENT PEER BEHAVIORS
     (Check those that apply)

More arguing_____

Less interest in play dates_____

Less communication with peers_____

Others_____
_____

RECOMMENDATIONS

Team conference_____

In-school individual counseling_____

In-school peer group counseling_____

Referral to counseling agency_____

Referral to support group_____

Testing_____

FOLLOW UP

Monthly Follow Up_____ Source_____Date_____

Information_____

PROFESSIONAL HELP

When any of the following are observed in a child, professional intervention may be helpful.

1. Child **continually** shares no thoughts or feelings about loss. *Tommy doesn't cry or talk about his mom's recent death.*

2. Child is **extremely** clingy to adults. *Tommy screams and cries. He is afraid to go to school and wants to stay home.*

3. Child has been **lied to** about loss. *Tommy was told his dad died of a heart attack. He overheard his dad had committed suicide.*

4. Child **threatens** to hurt him or her self. *Tommy tells his best friend that he wants to kill himself.*

5. Child **won't** socialize. *Tommy quits baseball, soccer, or riding bikes.*

6. Child becomes **involved** with drugs or alcohol. *Tommy's mom finds marijuana in his room.*

7. Child is **cruel** to animals or **physically abusive** to other children. *Tommy repeatedly kicks his dog and throws sticks at him.*

8. Child has had a very **difficult** relationship to the deceased. *Tommy's deceased dad was an alcoholic who physically abused him.*

9. Child shows **extremes** in not sleeping or eating. *Tommy has lost 10 pounds in three weeks. He wakes up crying at 2 a.m.*

10. Child is **failing** school. *Tommy got four F's and 5 N's on his report card.*

11. Child exhibits **sudden** unexplained change. *Tommy gets suspended from school for continually starting fights with other children.*

Children exhibit normal signs of loss and grief in many ways. It is the <u>extreme behaviors and intensity of feelings and actions</u> that signal outside intervention is needed.

SUGGESTIONS FOR PARENTS
SEEKING PROFESSIONAL HELP

1. **Use** word-of-mouth recommendations as a good source of referrals. These referrals can be made by a friend, physician, or guidance counselor.

2. **Seek** out professional mental health associations such as social work, psychology, or counseling associations that provide listings and referrals for loss and grief therapists.

3. **Meet** with the therapist first if possible to decide if he or she is right for your child. Counselors or therapists typically work with children using play therapy tools such as art, music, clay, and story-telling as well as dialogue to facilitate expression of feelings.

4. **Ask** questions of the counselors or therapists.

   How does he or she approach loss and grief issues?
   How long are sessions?
   What is the cost per session?
   How frequently are parents informed about or included in sessions?
   What are the limits of confidentiality?

Confidentiality is an important component of child therapy. If the child has been abused or has thoughts of hurting himself or herself or others, the parent needs to know. Otherwise, parents need to understand the therapist-child relationship as separate and unique. The child's thoughts and feelings need to remain private. Then parent and child both can gain a sense of respect for this valued relationship.

WE CAN MAKE A DIFFERENCE
BEFORE IT'S TOO LATE!

TO BEGIN, WE CAN

1. Identify the child who is dealing with a specific significant loss.

2. Recognize the grief and loss issue he or she is working through.

3. Realize his or her behaviors are "a cry for help." These behaviors are threatening to the system, yet they can be turned around if identified early.

4. Insist on getting help. How can a child learn in school and enjoy his or her day productively when he or she is carrying overwhelming feelings of grief?

5. Find resources—community, agencies, staff, peers.

6. Use team conferences as checks and balance system to safeguard a child's "right" to emotional help as well as intellectual help.

7. Develop an ***intra***-school data base where counselors can pool children within the same school with specific problems to connect with each other in peer groups.

8. Create an ***inter***-school data base to connect children in different schools together when none exist within their own school.

9. Reassure teachers that we can help. A panicked teacher can't create the environment a child needs to work through the hurt.

10. See the child differently. Expand time. Wait ten extra seconds to talk. Talk less. Be with him or her more. Let children tell you where they are, why they are there, and what they need. Have faith in them. Trust their perceptions. They are the only ones that really understand what they are going through. Let them explore and express in freedom.

Chapter 7

COMMUNITY AND NATIONAL RESOURCES POINT THE WAY TO HELP

COMMUNITY RESOURCES
FOR CHILDREN'S GRIEF AND LOSS ISSUES

Mental health agencies

Hospice programs

Funeral service professionals

Pediatricians

Clergy

School counselors

School psychologists

Pupil personnel workers

Nurses

Agencies or programs dealing with specific losses

AMERICA FOR A SOUND AIDS POLICY (ASAP)
P.O. BOX 17433
WASHINGTON, DC 20041
703 471-7350

ASSOCIATION FOR THE CARE OF CHILDREN'S HEALTH
7910 WOODMONT AVE.
BETHESDA, MD 20814
301 654-6549

ASSOCIATION FOR DEATH EDUCATION AND COUNSELING (ADEC)
638 PROSPECT AVE.
HARTFORD, CT 06105
203 232-4285

THE CANDLELIGHTERS
1312 18TH ST, N.W.
WASHINGTON, DC 20036
202 659-5136

CENTER FOR LOSS AND LIFE TRANSITION
3735 BROKEN ARROW RD.
FORT COLLINS, CO 80526
303 226-6050

CHILDRENS HOSPICE INTERNATIONAL
700 PRINCESS STREET, LOWER LEVEL
ALEXANDRIA, VA 22314
703-684-0330

COMPASSIONATE FRIENDS INC.
NATIONAL HEADQUARTERS
PO BOX 1347
OAK BROOK, IL 60521
312 323-5010

DOUGY'S PLACE
P.O. BOX 86852
PORTLAND, OR 97286
503 775-5683

DOWN'S SYNDROME SOCIETY
666 BROADWAY
SUITE 810
NEW YORK, NY 10012
800 221-2402

THE ELISABETH KUBLER-ROSS CENTER
SOUTH ROUTE 616
HEAD WATERS, VA 24442
703 396-3441

THE GOOD GRIEF PROGRAM
JUDGE BAKER GUIDANCE CENTER
295 LONGWOOD AVE.
BOSTON, MA 02115
617 232 8390

HOSPICE EDUCATION INSTITUTE
P.O. BOX 713
ESSEX, CT 06426-0713
800 331-1620   COMPUTURIZED "HOSPICE LINK"

MOTHERS AGAINST DRUNK DRIVING (MADD)
669 AIRPORT FREEWAY, SUITE 310
HURST, TX 76053
800 633-6233

NATIONAL ASSOCIATION FOR CHILDREN WITH AIDS
P.O. BOX 15485
DURHAM, NC 27704
919 477-5288

NATIONAL CENTER FOR MISSING & EXPLOITED CHILDREN
2101 WILSON BOULEVARD, SUITE 550
ARLINGTON, VA 22201-3052
703 235-3900

NATIONAL HOSPICE ORGANIZATION
1901 N. FT. MYER DRIVE
ARLINGTON, VA 22209
703 243-5900

NATIONAL SUDDEN INFANT DEATH SYNDROME FOUNDATION
105000 LITTLE PATUXENT PARKWAY, SUITE 420
COLUMBIA, MD 21044
800 221-SIDS

PARENTS OF MURDERED CHILDREN
1739 BELLA VISTA
CINCINNATI, OH 45237
513 721-LOVE

PARENTS WITHOUT PARTNERS
7910 WOODMONT AVE, SUITE 1000
BETHESDA, MD   20814
800 638-8078

PARENTS CAMPAIGN FOR HANDICAPPED CHILDREN AND YOUTH
CLOSER LOOK
BOX 1492
WASHINGTON, DC 20013
202 822-7900

PREGNANCY AND INFANT LOSS CENTER
1421 E. WAYZATA BLVD., SUITE 30
WAYZATA, MN 55391
612 473-9372

RESOLVE THRU SHARING
LACROSSE LUTHERAN HOSPITAL/GUNDERSEN CLINIC, LTD.
1910 SOUTH AVENUE
LACROSSE, WI 54601
608 791-4747

RONALD McDONALD HOUSE
419 EAST 86TH ST.
NEW YORK, NY 10028
212 876-1590

SHARE
PERINATAL NETWORK
ST. ELIZABETH'S HOSPITAL
211 SOUTH THIRD ST.
BELLEVILLE, IL 62222
314 947-6164

SIBLING SUPPORT CENTER
4800 SAND POINT WAY N.E.
P.O. BOX C5371
SEATTLE, WA 98105

ST. FRANCIS CENTER
5135 MACARTHUR BLVD., N.W.
WASHINGTON, DC 20016
202 363-8500

SIDS INFORMATION &
COUNSELING PROJECT
630 WEST FAYETTE ST.
ROOM 5684
BALTIMORE, MD 21201
410 706-5062

SURVIVORS OF SUICIDE
SUICIDE PREVENTION CENTER
184 SALEM AVE.
DAYTON, OH 45406
513 223-9096

ADVOCATES FOR CHILDREN AND YOUTH, INC.
300 CATHEDRAL ST., SUITE 500
BALTIMORE, MD 21201
410 547-9200

CALVERT HOSPICE
(KIDS' BEREAVEMENT GROUPS)
P.O. BOX 838
PRINCE FREDERICK, MD 20678

CARDINAL SHEEHAN CENTER-STELLA MARIS HOSPICE
("ME TOO!" CHILDREN'S BEREAVEMENT PROGRAM)
2300 DULANEY VALLEY ROAD
TOWSON, MD 21204
410 252-4500 EXT. 287

CENTER FOR LOSS AND GRIEF THERAPY
10400 CONNECTICUT AVE., SUITE 514
KENSINGTON, MD 20985
301 942-6440

CHILDREN OF SEPARATION AND DIVORCE, INC.
2000 CENTURY PLAZA #121
COLUMBIA, MD 21044
410 740-9553

CHILDREN'S HOME HEALTH CARE
111 MICHIGAN AVE., N.W.
WASHINGTON, DC 20010
202 939-4663

FAMILY SUPPORT CENTER
(KIDS' BEREAVEMENT GROUPS)
4308 MONTGOMERY AVE.
BETHESDA, MD 20814
301 718-2467

GRIEF CRISIS PROGRAM
FAIRFAX COUNTY
FAIRFAX, VA 22152
703 866-2100

THE GRIEF SUPPORT NETWORK
VIRGINIA ASSOCIATION FOR HOSPICES
7814 CAROUSEL LN., SUITE 300
RICHMOND, VA 23294
703 433-4427

HOWARD COUNTY SEXUAL ASSAULT CENTER
(KIDS' SUPPORT GROUPS)
GORMAN PLAZA BUILDING
8950 ROUTE 108, SUITE 124
COLUMBIA, MD 21045
410 964-0504

HOSPICE OF NORTHERN VA
6400 ARLINGTON BLVD.
SUITE 1000
FALLS CHURCH, VA   22042
703 534-7070

INSTITUTE FOR ATTITUDINAL STUDIES
P. O. BOX 19222
ALEXANDRIA, VA 22320

JUST FOR KIDS THE FAMILY LIFE CENTER
(KIDS' SUPPORT GROUP FOR HOMES WITH DRUGS AND ALCOHOL)
WILDE LAKE VILLIAGE GREEN
10451 TWIN RIVERS ROAD
COLUMBIA, MD 21044

THE MARYLAND COMMITTEE FOR CHILDREN
608 WATER STREET
BALTIMORE, MD   21202
410 752-7588

MEDICAL ILLNESS COUNSELING CENTER
CHEVY CHASE METRO BUILDING, SUITE 530
TWO WISCONSIN CIRCLE
CHEVY CHASE, MD   20815

MONTGOMERY COUNTY HOSPICE
(CHILDREN'S BEREAVEMENT GROUPS)
1450 RESEARCH BLVD
ROCKVILLE, MD   20850
301 279-2566

"MY FRIEND'S HOUSE"
(SUPPORT GROUPS FOR KIDS)
LIFE WITH CANCER
FAIRFAX HOSPITAL
3300 GALLOWS ROAD
FALLS CHURCH, VA 22046
703 698-2841

PARENT ENCOURAGEMENT CENTER
10100 CONNECTICUT AVE.
KENSINGTON, MD   20895
301 929-8824

ST. FRANCIS CENTER
5135 MACARTHUR BLVD., N.W.
WASHINGTON, DC 20016
202 363-8500

ST. JOHN'S COMMUNITY SERVICES
PRESCHOOL EARLY INTERVENTION PROGRAM
4880 MACARTHUR BLVD., N.W.
WASHINGTON, DC 20007
202 338-3726

STEVEN DANIEL JEFFREYS FOUNDATION, LTD.
GRIEF COUNSELING SERVICE
C/O FAMILY LIFE CENTER
WILDE LAKE VILLAGE GREEN
COLUMBIA, MD 21044
410 997-4884

WOMEN SUPORTING WOMEN: A BREAST CANCER SUPPORT GROUP
P O BOX 163
SALISBURY, MD 21803
410 749-1624

WISER (WASHINGTON INDEPENDENT SERVICES FOR EDUCATIONAL
RESOURCES)
P O BOX 7412
ARLINGTON, VA 22207
703 241-8166

Chapter **8**

LET'S EXPLORE MATERIALS:

THERE IS SOMETHING FOR EVERY LOSS

BOOKS

VIDEOS

MANUALS

GUIDES

CURRICULA

TODAY'S MATERIALS—A 90S UPDATE

Today as educators we are not alone. Many new and useful materials are available for children, teachers, counselors, and parents. These materials provide **practical** resources and information that you can use, as well as **state-of-the-art** literature of the 90s covering the spectrum of topics of grief and loss issues for children.

These materials are geared to different ages and different developmental levels, and often they stress that ideas designed to prepare children for and help children through inevitable loss must be **age appropriate.**

ANNOTATED
BIBLIOGRAPHY

ADULT RESOURCES THAT HELP

BOOKS

Bothun, Linda. (1987). *When Friends Ask about Adoption.* Chevy Chase, MD: Swan Publications. A useful question and answer guide on adoption for caring adults and nonadoptive parents.

Bradshaw, John. (1988). *The Family: A Revolutionary Way of Self Discovery.* Deerfield Beach, FL: Health Communications, Inc. An introspective view of family systems and inner child work.

Brett, Doris. (1986). *Annie Stories.* New York, NY: Workman Publishing. A series of stories that can be read to children under ten dealing with many childhood issues, such as death and divorce. The author provides advice for caring adults on how to use these stories.

Cassini, Kathleen, and Rogers, Jacqueline. (1990). *Death and the Classroom.* Cincinnati, OH: Griefwork of Cincinnati. A teacher's textbook that confronts death in the classroom.

Celotta, Beverly. (1991). *Generic Crisis Intervention Procedures.* Gaithersburg, MD: Beverly Celotta. A guide for youth suicide crisis intervention in school settings.

Coles, Robert. (1991). *The Spiritual Life of Children.* Boston, MA: Houghton Mifflin Co. A book sharing thoughts, drawings, and dreams that reflect the inner world of children.

Dass, Ram, and Gorman, Paul. (1985). *How Can I Help?* New York, NY: Alfred A. Knopf. A book of stories and reflections on service and how we can help with a loving heart.

DuPrau, Jeanne. (1981). *Adoption.* New York, NY: Julian Mesner. A series of different stories for young adults about facts and feelings related to adoption. It includes a list of helpful agencies.

Fitzgerald, Helen. (1992). *The Grieving Child.* New York, NY: Simon and Schuster. A wonderful guide for parents to use to help children work with their grief.

Fox, Sandra. (1988). *Good Grief: Helping Groups of Children When a Friend Dies.* Boston, MA: New England Association for the Education of Young Children. An excellent source of information for adults working with children whose friends have died.

Frankl, Victor. (1984). *Man's Search for Meaning.* New York, NY: Simon and Schuster. A powerful account of the author's imprisonment in Nazi Germany and the love that helped him survive his losses.

Furth, Gregg. (1988). *The Secret World of Drawings.* Boston, MA: Sigo Press. A comprehensive look at children's artwork and ways of understanding it.

Gibran, Kahlil. (1969). *The Prophet.* New York, NY: Alfred A. Knopf. A beautiful book of poetry expressing timeless feelings of life and death, pleasure and pain, and joy and sorrow.

Gil, Eliana. (1991). *The Healing Power of Play.* New York, NY: Guilford Publisher. This book gives a history of play therapy and specific considerations for working with abused and neglected children.

Ginsberg, Herbert, and Opper, Sylvia. (1976). *Piaget's Theory of Intellectual Development.* Englewood Cliffs, NJ: Prentice-Hall. A thorough look at Piaget's theory of development.

Gliko-Braden, Majel. (1992). *Grief Comes to Class.* Omaha, NE: Centering Corporation. This book is meant to help teachers and parents assist bereaved children.

Grollman, Earl. (1967). *Explaining Death to Children.* Boston, MA: Beacon Press. A book geared to adults who want to ease a child's first confrontation with the death of a loved one.

Heavilin, Marilyn. (1986). *Roses in December.* San Bernardino, CA: Here's Life Publishers. The author expresses a deep understanding of the grieving process, having experienced the death of three children.

Huntley, Theresa. (1991). *Helping Children Grieve When Someone They Love Dies.* Minneapolis, MN: Augsburg Fortress. An easy-to-read resource for caring adults that honestly addresses children's grief.

Ilse, Sherokee. (1982). *Empty Arms.* Maple Plain, MN: Wintergreen Press. This is a practical book for anyone who has experienced infant death or miscarriage. It offers suggestions and support for decision making at the time of loss and future concerns and grief work.

Johnson, Sherry. (1987). *After a Child Dies: Counseling Bereaved.* New York, NY: Springer Publishing Inc. A comprehensive text that offers information on counseling bereaved families when a child dies.

Kubler-Ross, Elisabeth. (1975). *On Death and Dying.* Englewood, NJ: Prentice-Hall. A pioneering book on the subject of death and dying, using real-life situations to create true understanding.

Kubler-Ross, Elisabeth. (1985). *On Children and Dying.* New York, NY: Macmillan. Elisabeth Kubler-Ross offers the families of dead and dying children honest information, helpful ideas, and strength to cope.

Kushner, Harold. (1981). *When Bad Things Happen to Good People.* New York, NY: Avon Books. Rabbi Kushner shares his thoughts and feelings of why we suffer. The book was written following his son's illness and subsequent death.

Leon, Irving. (1990). *When a Baby Dies.* New Haven, CT: Yale University Press. The first book to explore therapeutically the loss of a baby during pregnancy or as a newborn. It addresses the subject of surviving siblings.

Levine, Stephen. (1987). *Healing into Life and Death.* New York, NY: Anchor Press. Stephen Levine explores ways to open our hearts to healing.

Linn, Erin. (1990). *150 Facts about Grieving Children.* Incline Village, NV: The Publisher's Mark. A series of 150 paragraphs discussing important information and understandings about the grieving child.

Miller, Alice. (1984). *For Your Own Good.* New York, NY: Farrar, Straus, and Giroux. Alice Miller deeply explores the repercussions of adults taking over a child's will.

Mills, G., Reisler R., Robinson, A., and Vermilye, G. (1976). *Discussing Death.* Palm Springs, CA: ETC Publication. A guide for death education giving practical suggestions and resources for many age levels.

Moustakas, Clark. (1992). *Psychotherapy with Children.* Greeley, CO: Carron Publishers. A classic text in understanding the therapeutic environment.

Oaklander, Violet. (1969). *Windows to Our Children: Gestalt Therapy for Children.* New York, NY: Center for Gestalt Development. A Gestalt Therapy approach to children's loss and grief work with stories and practical suggestions for play therapy.

Peck, Scott. (1978). *The Road Less Traveled.* New York, NY: Simon and Schuster Inc. Scott Peck explores traditional values and spiritual growth through a new psychology of love.

Quackenbush, Jamie, and Graveline, Denise. (1985). *When Your Pet Dies.* New York, NY: Pocket Books. A book for pet owners to help understand feelings when a pet dies.

Rando, Theresa. (1988). *How to Go On Living When Someone You Love Dies.* New York, NY: Lexington Books. A helpful and informative book addressing grief and how to work with it.

Siegel, Bernie. (1986). *Love, Medicine and Miracles.* New York, NY: Harper and Row Publishers. A book that emphasizes recognizing how our mind influences our body and how to use that knowledge for healing.

Smilansky, Sara. (1987). *On Death (Helping Children Understand and Cope).* New York, NY: Peter Lang. The author bases her studies on children and their grief process in Tel Aviv.

Trout, Susan. (1990). *To See Differently.* Washington DC: Three Roses Press. This is an excellent book to help readers heal their minds after experiencing many life issues. A chapter on working with feelings about death is included.

Wolfelt, Alan. (1983). *Helping Children Cope with Grief.* Muncie, IN: Accelerated Development Inc. An informative resource for caring adults working with bereaved children. Includes ideas for leading discussions.

Wolfelt, Alan. (1992). *Sarah's Journey.* Fort Collins, CO: Center for Loss and Life Transition. Eight-year-old Sarah's father suddenly died. Dr. Wolfelt presents three years of Sarah's grief experience and provides counseling perspectives and guidelines for caring adults.

Worden, J. William. (1983). *Grief Counseling and Grief Therapy.* New York, NY: Springer Publishing. A comprehensive handbook for grief counseling.

A PERSON IS A PERSON,
NO MATTER HOW SMALL.

BY DR. SEUSS

VIDEOS

A Child's View of Grief. Alan Wolfelt. (1991). Fort Collins, CO: Center for Loss and Life Transition. A 20-minute video with real children and parents sharing stories and emotions.

A Family in Grief: The Ameche Story. (1989). Champagne, IL: Research Press. A real family story of bereavement with guide included.

Dougy's Place: A 20-20 Video. (1992). Portland, OR: The Dougy Center. A candid look at the kids participating in the Dougy Center's program.

What Do I Tell My Children? (1992). Leslie Kussman. Wellesley, MA: Aquarian Productions. A film narrated by Joanne Woodward showing experts, adults, and children exploring their thoughts and feelings regarding death.

When Grief Comes to School. (1991). Carol and David Ebeling. Bloomington, IN: Blooming Educational Enterprises. A film and manual showing families and school personnel discussing grief issues.

CURRICULA AND MANUALS

Lagorio, Jeanne. (1991). *Life Cycle Education Manual.* Solana Beach, CA: Empowerment in Action. A teacher's guide to help with loss issues including specific lesson plans and guided book activities.

O'Toole, Donna. (1989). *Growing through Grief.* Burnsville, NC: Mt. Rainbow Publications, Burnsville. A K-12 curriculum to help children through loss.

BOOK SERVICES

Centering Corporation. Omaha, NE. A service offering resources on topics of loss and grief for children.

Child'swork Child'splay. King of Prussia, PA. A catalogue that addresses the mental health needs of children, parents, and counselors.

Compassion Book Service and *Mt. Rainbow Publications.* Burnsville, NC. A service offering books for and about children.

Waterfront Books Publishing Co. Burlington, VT. A service offering books that support children and the adults in their lives.

Wintergreen Press. Maple Plain, MN. A resource for materials relating to grief associated with miscarriage, stillborn, and infant death.

BOOKS ABOUT DEATH

Brown, Margaret Wise. (1979). *The Dead Bird.* New York, NY: Dell Publishing. A story of four children who find a dead bird, bury it, and hold a funeral service. Ages 4-8.

Campbell, James A. (1992). *The Secret Places.* Omaha, NE: Centering Corporation. The story of Ryan and his journey through grief is for children and adults to gain an in-depth look at childhood grief. Ages 6-12.

Dodge, Nancy. (1984). *Thumpy's Story: The Story of Grief and Loss Shared by Thumpy the Bunny.* Springfield, IL: Prairie Lark Press. The story of the death of Thumpy's sister, who was not strong enough to keep living. Ages 5-12.

Ferguson, Dorothy. (1992). *A Bunch of Balloons.* Omaha, NE: Centering Corporation. A resource to help grieving children understand loss and remember what they have left after someone dies. Ages 5-8.

Kolf, June Cerza. (1990). *Teenagers Talk about Grief.* Grand Rapids, MI: Baker Book House. A book written especially for and about teenage grief with an account of firsthand experiences. For teens.

Oehler, Jerri. (1978). *The Frog Family's Baby Dies*. Durham, NC: Duke University Medical Center. A coloring storybook for very young children discussing sibling loss. Ages 3-6.

O'Toole, Donna. (1988). *Aardy Aardvark Finds Hope*. (Adult manual available) Burnsville: NC: Mt. Rainbow Publications . The story of animals that present the pain, sadness, and eventual hope after death. Ages 5-8.

Scravani, Mark. (1988). *Love, Mark*. Syracuse, NY: Hope For Bereaved. Letters written to grieving children to help them express feelings. Ages 7-12.

Varley, Susan. (1984). *Badger's Parting Gifts*. New York, NY: Morrow and Co. Badger was a special friend to all the animals. After his death, each friend recalls a special memory of Badger. All ages.

White, E.B. (1952). *Charlotte's Web*. New York, NY: Harper and Row. Through the eyes of the farm animals, life and death are sweetly portrayed. Ages 8-13.

BOOKS ABOUT DEATH OF A PET

Carrick, Carol. (1976). *The Accident*. New York, NY: Clarion Books. Christopher's dog is killed by a truck. Christopher deals with his feelings as he prepares to bury his dog.

Cohen, Miriam. (1984). *Jim's Dog Muffin*. New York, NY: Dell Publishing. Jim's dog Muffin is killed and everyone in his first-grade class is sad and tries to help him feel better. Ages 5-8.

Montgomery, H., and Montgomery, M. (1991). *Good-Bye My Friend*. Minneapolis, MN: Montgomery Press. A series of vignettes honoring the grief involved with the death of a pet. Suggestions on commemorating and remembering animals are included. Ages 8-13.

Rogers, Fred. (1988). *When a Pet Dies*. New York, NY: G.P. Putnam Sons. A first experience book using photographs and words to show what we can do and feel when a pet dies. Ages 4-7.

Sanford, Doris. (1985). *It Must Hurt a Lot.* Portland, OR: Multnomah Press. A boy learns to express his emotions and hold fondly his memories after his dog is killed. Ages 4-10.

Stein, Sarah. (1974). *About Dying.* New York, NY: Walker and Co. Simple text and photographs to help young children understand death, including a discussion about children's feelings for adults. Ages 3-6.

Viorst, Judith. (1971). *The Tenth Good Thing about Barney.* New York, NY: Atheneum. The story of a pet cat that dies and how we can use funerals and other ways of commemorating with children. Ages 4-8.

BOOKS ABOUT PARENTS DYING

Blume, Judy. (1981). *Tiger Eyes.* New York, NY: Macmillan Children's Group. Fifteen-year-old Davey works through the feelings of his father's murder in a store hold-up. Ages 11 and up.

Douglas, Eileen. (1990). *Rachel and the Upside Down Heart.* Los Angeles, CA: Price Stern Sloan. The true story of four-year-old Rachel, and how her father's death affects her life. Ages 5-9.

Frost, Dorothy. (1991). *DAD! Why'd You Leave Me?* Scottdale, PA: Herald Press. This is a story about ten-year-old Ronnie who can't understand why his dad died. Ages 8-12.

Greenfield, Eloise. (1993). *Nathanial Talking.* New York, NY: Black Butterfly Children's Group. Nathanial, an energetic nine-year-old, helps us understand a black child's world after his mom dies. He uses rap and rhyme to express his feelings. Ages 7-11.

Krementz, Jill. (1981). *How It Feels When a Parent Dies.* New York, NY: Knoph Publishing Co. Eighteen children (ages 7-16) speak openly words about their feelings and experiences after the death of a parent.

Lanton, Sandy. (1991). *Daddy's Chair.* Rockville, MD: Kar-Ben Copies Inc. Michael's dad died. The book follows the Shiva, the Jewish week of mourning. He doesn't want anyone to sit in Daddy's chair. Ages 5-10.

LeShan, Eda. (1975). *Learning to Say Goodbye When a Parent Dies.* New York, NY: Macmillan Publishing Co. Written directly to children about problems to be recognized and overcome when a parent dies. Ages 8 and up.

Levine, Jennifer. (1992). *Forever in My Heart.* Burnsville, NC: Mt. Rainbow Publications. A story and workbook that helps children participate in life when their parent is dying. Ages 5-9.

Powell, E. Sandy. (1990). *Geranium Morning.* Minneapolis, MN: Carol Rhoda Books, Inc. A boy's dad is killed in a car accident and a girl's mom is dying. The children share their feelings within a special friendship. Ages 6 and up.

Tiffault, Benette. (1992). *A Quilt for Elizabeth.* Omaha, NE: Centering Corporation, Inc. Elizabeth's grandmother helps her understand her feelings after her father dies. This is a good story to initiate an open dialogue with children. Ages 7 and up.

Thaut, Pamela. (1991). *Spike and Ben.* Deerfield Beach, FL: Health Communications Inc. The story of a boy whose friend's mom dies. Ages 5-8.

Vigna, Judith. (1991). *Saying Goodbye to Daddy.* Niles, IL: Albert Whitman and Co. A sensitive story about a dad's death and the healing that takes place in the weeks that follow. Ages 5-8.

BOOK ABOUT A PARENT COMMITTING SUICIDE

Urich, Jeanette. (1990). *I Wish I were in a Lonely Meadow: When a Parent Commits Suicide.* Portland, OR: Dougy Center. This book is a compilation of children's own writings about their experience with a parent's suicide. Ages 9-15.

BOOKS ABOUT A SIBLING'S DEATH

Alexander, Sue. (1983). *Nadia the Willful.* New York, NY: Pantheon Books. Nadia's older brother dies, and she helps her father heal his grief by willfully talking about her brother. Ages 6-10.

Erling, Jake, and Erling, Susan. (1986). *Our Baby Died. Why?* Maple Plain, MN: Pregnancy and Infant Loss Center. A little boy shares his thoughts and feelings about the birth of his stillborn brother and eventual birth of sibling twins. Children can read, draw, and color. Ages 4-10.

Gryte, Marilyn. (1991). *No New Baby.* Omaha, NE: Centering Corporation. Siblings are allowed to express their feelings about mom's miscarriage. Ages 5-8.

Johnson, Joy, and Johnson, Marv. (1982). *Where's Jess?* Omaha, NE: Centering Corporation. A book for young children that addresses the questions and feelings kids have when a sibling dies. Ages 4-7.

Linn, Erin. (1982). *Children Are Not Paperdolls.* Springfield, IL: Human Services Press. Kids who have had brothers and sisters die draw and comment on their experiences. Ages 8-12.

Richter, Elizabeth. (1986). *Losing Someone You Love: When a Brother or Sister Dies.* New York, NY: Putnam Publishing Group. Adolescents share feelings and experiences about the death of a sibling. Ages 11 and up.

Romond, Janis. (1989). *Children Facing Grief.* St. Meinrad, IN: Abbey Press. Letters from bereaved brothers and sisters, telling of their experiences and offering hope. Ages 6-14.

Sims, Alicia. (1986). *Am I Still a Sister?* Slidell, LA: Big A and Co. This story was written by an eleven-year-old who experienced her baby brother's death. Ages 8-12.

Temes, Roberta. (1992). *The Empty Place.* Far Hills, NJ: Small Horizons. The story of a third grade boy whose older sister dies. Ages 5-9.

BOOKS ABOUT A FRIEND'S DEATH

Blackburn, Lynn. (1987). *Timothy Duck.* Omaha, NE: Centering Corporation. Timothy Duck's friend John gets sick and dies. Timothy Duck shares his feelings with others. Ages 5-8.

Blackburn, Lynn. (1991). *The Class in Room 44.* Omaha, NE: Centering Corporation. The children in Room 44 share their feelings of grief when their classmate Tony dies. Ages 6-10.

Cohen, Janice. (1987). *I Had a Friend Named Peter.* New York, NY: William Morrow and Co. Betsy's friend Peter dies suddenly. She learns through parents and teachers that Peter's memory can live on. Ages 5-10.

Kaldhol, M., and Wenche, O. (1987). *Goodbye Rune.* New York, NY: Kane-Miller. A story about the drowning death of a girl's best friend and how parents can help. Ages 5-12.

Kubler-Ross, Elisabeth. (1987). *Remember the Secret.* Berkeley, CA: Celestial Arts. The imaginative story of love and faith of two children, and their experience with death. Ages 5-10.

BOOKS ABOUT A GRANDPARENT'S DEATH

Fassler, Joan. (1983). *My Grandpa Died Today.* Springfield, IL: Human Sciences Press. David did not fear death as much because Grandpa knew that David would have the courage to live. Ages preschool to 7.

Holden, L. Dwight. (1989). *Gran-Gran's Best Trick.* New York, NY: Magination Press. This book deals directly with cancer. It follows the treatment, sickness, and death of a grandparent. Ages 6-12.

Pomerantz, Barbara. (1983). *Bubby, Me, and Memories.* New York, NY: Union Of American Hebrew Congregations. A child's grandmother dies. The child's feelings are addressed and his questions answered. Good source to explain Jewish rituals. Ages 5-8.

Thomas, Jane. (1988). *Saying Good-bye to Grandma.* New York, NY: Clarion Books. A sensitively written book about a family's joining together for grandma's funeral. Ages 5-10.

Thornton, Terence. (1987). *Grandpa's Chair.* Portland, OR: Multnomah Press. The story of a small boy's love for his grandfather, his last visit to see him, and his grandfather's eventual death. Ages 4-8.

BOOKS ABOUT WAR/DEATH

Bunting, Eve. (1990). *The Wall.* New York, NY: Clarion Books. Illustrations and story about a father and son who visit the Vietnam Veterans Memorial and the impact of war on three generations. Ages 5-8.

Coerr, Eleanor. (1977). *Sadako and the Thousand Paper Cranes.* New York, NY: Putnam Publishing Group. This is a true story about a Japanese girl who is dying from her exposure to radiation from the bomb at Hiroshima. Her hope for peace and life is symbolized in her paper cranes. Ages 8-13.

WORKBOOKS ON DEATH FOR CHILDREN

Boulden, Jim, and Boulden, Joan. (1991). *Saying Goodbye.* Santa Rosa, CA: Boulden Publishing. A bereavement workbook and coloring book for young children. Ages 5-8.

Haasl, Beth, and Marnocha, Jean. (1990). *Bereavement Support Group Program for Children.* Muncie, IN: Accelerated Development Inc. A step-by-step workbook for children with leader manual to use in a bereavement group. Ages 8-13.

Hammond, Janice. (1980). *When My Mommy Died* or *When My Daddy Died.* Flint, MI: Cranbrook Publishing. Both workbooks are geared to young children's bereavement work and parent death.

Heegaard, Marge. (1988). *When Someone Very Special Dies.* Minneapolis, MN: Woodland Press. An excellent workbook that uses artwork and journaling to allow children to work through their grief. A facilitator's manual is available. Ages 5-12.

Rogers, Fred. (1991). *So Much to Think about.* Pittsburgh, PA: Family Communications, Inc. An activity book for young children when someone they love has died. Ages 5-8.

Traisman, Enid Samuel. (1992). *Fire in My Heart; Ice in My Veins.* Omaha, NE: Centering Corporation. A wonderful workbook for teenagers to explore thoughts and feelings and record grief memories. For teenagers.

SPECIAL MEMORY BOOK

Braza, Kathleen. (1988). *Memory Book: For Bereaved Children.* Salt Lake City, UT: Healing Resources. A workbook for bereaved children to express their feelings through drawing and writing. Ages 5-11.

Chimeric, Inc. (1991). *Illustory.* Denver, CO. Kids can write and illustrate their own books that can be sent away and made into hardcover bound books with the original texts. Ages 5-10.

Sibbilt, Sally. (1991). *Oh, Where Has My Pet Gone?* Wayzata, MN: B. Libby Press. A pet loss memory book that uses writing and drawing to help children commemorate a pet's death. Ages 5-12.

BOOKS ABOUT LIFE CYCLES

Buscaglia, Leo. (1982). *The Fall of Freddie the Leaf.* Thorofare, NJ: Charles B. Slack Co. The story of the changing seasons as a metaphor for life and death. Ages 4-8.

Gerstein, Mordica. (1987). *The Mountains of Tibet.* New York, NY: Harper and Row. The story of a woodcutter's journey from the mountains of Tibet through the universe of endless choices and back to his home again. Ages 7 and up.

Hoban, Tana. (1971). *Look Again.* New York, NY: Macmillan Publishing Co. A book of photographs that illustrates to children we can't always know the larger picture when we see only one small part. Ages 4-7.

Mellonie, Bryan, and Ingpen, Robert. (1983). *Lifetimes: The Beautiful Way to Explain Death to Children.* New York, NY: Bantam Books. Explains the ongoing life cycle of plants, animals, and people. Ages 3-10.

Munsch, Robert. (1983). *Love You Forever.* Willowdale, Canada: A Firefly Book. A beautiful book for adults and children alike about the continuance of love throughout life. All ages.

Wood, Douglas. (1992). *Old Turtle*. Duluth, MN: Pfeifer-Hamilton. A fable for children and adults that captures the message of peace on earth and oneness with nature. The illustrations are beautiful. Ages 5 and up.

BOOKS ON AGING GRANDPARENTS

De Paola, Tommie. (1980). *Now One Foot, Now the Other*. New York, NY: G.P. Putnam's Sons. The story of a grandfather's stroke and how it affects his grandchildren. Ages 5-8.

Farber, Norma. (1979). *How Does It Feel to Be Old?* New York, NY: E. P. Dutton. A grandmother talks about how she feels to be old. A good book for grandparents and grandchildren to share. Ages 6-12.

Miles, Miska. (1971). *Annie and the Old One*. Boston, MA: Joy Street Books. A Navaho girl's aging grandmother gets ready to die. Annie attempts to undo the weaving of a rug to stop this dying process. Ages 7-12.

Nelson, Vacinda. (1988). *Always Grandma*. New York, NY: South China Printing Co. A grandmother develops Alzheimer's disease and her grandchild learns to live with grandmother's present condition and hold memories of her when she was healthy. Ages 5-8.

BOOKS ABOUT ADULT ILLNESS

Goodman, Michael B. (1991). *Vanishing Cookies*. Mississauga, Canada: Arthur Jones Lithographing Ltd. A book that talks honestly about a parent's cancer treatment. Ages 6-13.

Heegaard, Marge. (1991). *When Someone Has a Very Special Illness.* Minneapolis, MN: Woodland Press. Practical workbook that addresses feelings when a parent is sick. Children can illustrate it themselves. Ages 6-12.

LeShan, Eda. (1986). *When a Parent Is Very Sick.* Boston, MA: Joy Street Books. A helpful book for children and parents that talks openly about the stress of having a parent with a serious illness. Ages 8-13.

Nystrom, Caroline. (1990). *Emma Says Goodbye.* Batavia, IL: Lion Publisher. Emma's aunt has a terminal illness, and she comes to live with Emma. Ages 8-14.

Parkinson, Carolyn. (1991). *My Mommy Has Cancer.* Rochester, NY: Park Press. This book helps young children learn about cancer, its treatment, and its emotional impact. Ages 4-8.

Strauss, Linda. (1988). *Coping When a Parent Has Cancer.* New York, NY: Rosen Publishing. A book for teenagers who are coping with a parent with cancer. For teenagers.

BOOKS ABOUT CHILDREN'S ILLNESS

Baznik, Donna. (1981). *Becky's Story.* Bethesda, MD: ACCH Publisher. Becky, a six-year-old, feels confused and left out when her brother is in a bad accident and she feels he is given all the attention. Ages 4-7.

Gaes, Jason. (1988) *My Book for Kids with Cansur.* Pierre, SD: Melius-Peterson. The story of eight-year-old Jason who successfully battles cancer. Jason's brothers illustrated the book. Ages 7-12.

Lawrence, Melinda. (1987). *My Life: Melinda's Story.* Alexandria, VA: Children's Hospice International. A story by Melinda and her journey through illness. Ages 5 and up.

Maple, Marilyn. (1992). *On the Wings of a Butterfly.* Seattle, WA: Parenting Press. A butterfly becomes a friend to Lisa, a child dying of cancer. She shares her fears of dying. Ages 5-10.

Kubler-Ross, Elisabeth. (1979). *Dougy's Letter.* Head Waters, VA: Elisabeth Kubler-Ross Center. Elisabeth Kubler-Ross writes a wonderful letter to Dougy, a child with cancer. All ages.

Schultz. Charles M. (1990). *Why, Charlie Brown, Why?* New York, NY: Topper Books. The story about Charlie's friend Janice, who has leukemia, and what happens when a friend is very ill. Ages 5-10.

Stolp, Hans. (1990). *The Golden Bird.* New York, NY: Dial Books. An eleven-year-old boy is terminally ill and explores his thoughts and feelings about death. Ages 9-14.

BOOKS ABOUT DOWN'S SYNDROME

Cairo, Shelley, Cairo, Jasmine, and Cairo, Tara. (1985). *Our Brother Has Down's Syndrome.* Ontario, Canada: Annick Press LTD. A loving book that explains Down's Syndrome to young children through facts and photographs. Ages 5-8.

O'Shaughnessy, Ellen. (1992). *Somebody Called Me a Retard Today . . . and My Heart Felt Sad.* New York, NY: Walker and Co. A lovely book explaining in a very simple way how a young mentally challenged girl feels when she is confronted with being different. Ages 5-adult.

BOOKS ABOUT AIDS

Hausherr, Rosmarie. (1989). *Children and the AIDS Virus.* New York, NY: Clarion Books. An informative book for older and younger children that tells and shows through pictures the world of AIDS. Ages 5 and up.

Jordan, MaryKate. (1989). *Losing Uncle Tim.* Niles, IL: A. Whitman Niles. Daniel's Uncle Tim dies of AIDS, and he struggles with many feelings about it. Ages 7-11.

Merrifield, Margaret. (1990). *Come Sit by Me*. Ontario, Canada: Women's Press. A great book for parents and teachers to educate young children on the facts about AIDS. Ages 4-8.

Sanford, Doris. (1991). *David Has AIDS*. Portland, OR: Multnomah Press. David struggles with the disease of AIDS. Ages 7-11.

BOOKS ABOUT ASTHMA

Rogers, Allison. (1987). *Luke Has Asthma*. Burlington, VT: Waterfront Books. The story of Luke and his life with asthma. Ages 3-7.

BOOKS ABOUT WEIGHT DISORDERS AND EATING PROBLEMS

Berry, Joy. (1990). *About Weight Problems and Eating Disorders*. Chicago, IL: Children's Press. An interesting book that explains the realities of eating disorders and weight problems. Ages 7-13.

BOOKS ABOUT CHILDHOOD DIABETES

Betschart, Jean. (1991). *A Workbook on Diabetes for Children*. Minneapolis, MN: DCI publishing. This is an easy-to-understand workbook for children to help them manage diabetes. Ages 6-12.

Mulder, Linnea. (1992). *Sarah and Puffle*. New York, NY: Magination Press. A book to help children and their family cope with diabetes. Ages 5-9.

BOOKS ABOUT CHILDREN WHO STOP GROWING

Russo, Marisabina. (1990). *Alex Is My Friend*. New York, NY: Greenwillow Books. The story of a boy whose good friend is a dwarf. The boy realizes that although his friend does not grow, their friendship deepens through time and they continue to have fun together. Ages 5-8.

BOOKS ABOUT STRANGER ANXIETY AND/OR ELECTIVE MUTISM

Schaefer, Charles. (1992). *Cat's Got Your Tongue*. New York, NY: Magination Press. This is the story of Anna, a kindergartner diagnosed as an electively mute child. Children with stranger anxieties also can relate to Anna's behaviors. Ages 3-7.

BOOKS ABOUT MOVING

Blume, Judy. (1986). *Are You There God? It's Me Margaret*. New York, NY: Dell Publishing. Margaret has to face moving and beginning a new life. Especially good for girls in grades 3 through 7.

McKend, Heather. (1988). *Moving Gives Me a Stomachache*. Ontario, Canada: Black Moss Press. The story of a child's anxiety and fear of moving. Ages 5-8.

BOOKS ABOUT DIVORCE

Boulden, Jim, and Boulden, Joan. (1991). *Let's Talk.* Santa Rosa, CA: Boulden Publishing. A kid's activity book for separation and divorce. Ages 5-8.

Evans, Marla D. (1989). *This Is Me and My Single Parent.* New York, NY: Magination Press. A discovery workbook for children and single parents. Ages 8-13.

Fassler, D., Lash, M., and Ives, S. (1988). *Changing Families.* Burlington, VT: Waterfront Books. Advice for parents and children on coping with divorce, remarriage, and new families. Ages 4-12.

Heegaard, Marge. (1990). *When Mom and Dad Separate.* Minneapolis, MN: Woodland Press. A workbook for children exploring thoughts and feelings about separation and divorce. Ages 6-12.

Krementz, Jill. (1988). *How It Feels When Parents Divorce.* New York, NY: Knoph. Many different kinds of children describe how the divorce of their parents has affected them. Ages 8-13.

Sanford, Doris. (1985). *Please Come Home.* Portland, OR: Multnomah Press. Jenny's thoughts and feelings are expressed to her teddy bear about her parents' divorce. Ideas for adults to help children are included. Ages 7-12.

BOOKS ABOUT ADOPTION

Banish, R., and Jordan-Wong, J. (1992). *A Forever Family.* New York, NY: Harper Collins. Eight-year-old Jennifer was in many foster homes before being adopted as a part of her forever family. Ages 5-8.

Girard, Linda. (1989). *We Adopted You Benjamin Koo.* Niles, IL: A. Whitman and Co. Benjamin is a nine-year-old boy from another country. He tells of how he adjusted to adoption and a culturally blended family. Ages 6-9.

Sanford, Doris. (1989). *Brian Was Adopted.* Portland, OR: Multnomah Press. Brian questions many parts of adoption and talks to God about it. Ages 7-11.

Stinson, Kathy. (1992). *Steven's Baseball Mitt.* Ontario, Canada: Annick Press Ltd. The thoughts and feelings that go through an adopted child's mind about his birth mother. Ages 5-8.

BOOKS ABOUT DRUGS

Taylor, Clark. (1992). *The House that Crack Built.* San Francisco, CA: Chronicle Books. A poetic story for young children that explores today's drug problems. Ages 7-12.

BOOKS ABOUT SEXUAL ABUSE

Girard, Linda. (1984). *My Body Is Private.* Morton Grove, Il. Albert Whitman and Co. A direct approach to help children distinguish between good touching and bad touching, including help for parents. Ages 5-10.

Sanford, Doris. (1986). *I Can't Talk about It.* Portland, OR: Multnomah Press. Annie talks to an abstract form, Love, about her sexual abuse, and begins to heal and trust. Ages 8-13.

BOOKS ABOUT VIOLENCE IN THE HOME

Davis, Diane. (1984). *Something Is Wrong in My House.* Seattle, WA: Parenting Press, Inc. A book about parents fighting, ways to cope with violence, and how to break the cycle. Ages 8-12.

Paris, Susan. (1986). *Mommy and Daddy Are Fighting.* Seattle, WA: Seals Press. Honest discussion of parental fighting with a guide for parents. Ages 5-8.

Winston-Hiller, Randy. (1986). *Some Secrets Are for Sharing.* Denver, CO: MAC Publishing. A story of a family secret of a boy being beaten by his mom. He finally tells and gets help for himself and his mom. Ages 6-11.

BOOKS ABOUT TRAUMA

Berry, Joy. (1990). *About Traumatic Experiences.* Chicago, IL: Children's Press. Answers to kids' questions about trauma and traumatic experiences. Ages 8-11.

Nasta, Phyliss. (1991). *Aaron Goes to the Shelter.* Tucson, AZ: Whole Child. A story and workbook about children who have experienced family chaos and may be placed in a shelter or foster care. Ages 6-12.

BOOKS ABOUT NATURAL DISASTER

Williams, Vera. (1992). *A Chair for My Mother.* New York, NY: Mulberry Books. After a fire destroys their home, Rosa, her mom, and her grandmother save their money for a big chair to share. Ages 5-10.

BOOKS ABOUT FAMILIES WITH ALCOHOLICS

Black, Claudia. (1982). *"My Dad Loves Me, My Dad Has a Disease."* Denver, CO: MAC Publishing. This is a workbook for children of alcoholics to help them better understand alcoholism and their feelings about it. Ages 6-14.

Carbone, Elisa Lynn. (1992). *"My Dad's Definitely Not a Drunk."* Burlington, VT: Waterfront Books. Corey is a 12-year-old boy that struggles with a secret that his dad drinks too much. Corey and his mom discover a way to get help. Ages 9-14.

Hastings, Jill, and Typpo, Marion. (1984). *An Elephant in the Living Room.* Minneapolis, MN: Comp Care Publishers. A workbook about alcoholism that allows children to express their feelings. Ages 8-12.

Sanford, Doris. (1984). *I Know the World's Worst Secret.* Portland, OR: Multnomah Press. A girl talks about her alcoholic mom. Ages 8-13.

BOOKS ABOUT DADS

Cochran, Vicki. (1992). *My Daddy Is a Stranger.* Omaha, NE: Centering Corporation. The story of a little girl whose dad left home when she was a baby and how she feels and explains his absence. Ages 5-8.

Hickman, Martha. (1990). *When Andy's Father Went to Prison.* Niles, IL: Albert Whitman and Co. Andy's dad was arrested for stealing and put into prison. Andy copes with his feelings of shame and abandonment while his dad's away. Ages 5-9.

BOOKS ABOUT WORKING PARENTS

Molnar, Dorothy, and Fenton, Stephanie. (1991). *Who Will Pick Me Up When I Fall?* Niles, IL: Albert Whitman and Co. A little girl has difficulty remembering where she goes everyday while both parents are working. Ages 5-8.

Quinlan, Patricia. (1987). *My Dad Takes Care of Me.* Ontario, Canada: Annick Press. The story about a child who has a working mom, and a dad who stays home because he doesn't have a job. Ages 5-8.

BOOKS ABOUT IMMIGRATION

Fassler, David, and Danworth, Kimberly (1992). *Coming to America: The Kids' Book about Immigration.* Burlington, VT: Waterfront Books. A book created to help children share and explore their feelings about immigration. Ages 4-12.

BOOKS ABOUT ATTENTION DEFICIT HYPERACTIVITY DISORDER

Quinn, Patricia, and Stern, Judith. (1991). *Putting on the Brakes.* New York, NY: Magination Press. A guide for children to understand and work with ADHD. Ages 8-13.

BOOKS ABOUT DYSLEXIA

Janover, Caroline. (1988). *Josh: A Boy with Dyslexia.* Burlington, VT: Waterfront Books. The story about Josh and how he feels about having dyslexia. Ages 8-12.

BOOKS ABOUT FEELINGS

Blackburn, Lynn. (1991). *I Know I Made It Happen.* Omaha, NE: Centering Corporation. This book presents different circumstances where children find themselves feeling guilty and responsible for making things happen. Ages 5-8.

Crary, Elizabeth. (1992). *I'm Mad* or *I'm Frustrated.* Seattle, WA: Parenting Press. A series of children's books that identify feelings and gives options on what to do with them. Ages 3-8.

Doleski, Teddi. (1983). *The Hurt.* Mahwah, NJ: Paulest Press. The wonderful story about a little boy who keeps all of his hurts inside, until the hurt grows so big it fills his room. When he shares his feelings, the hurt begins to go away. All ages.

Hazen, Barbara. (1992). *Even if I Did Something Awful.* New York, NY: Aladdin Books. The reassuring story of a little girl that realizes mom will love her no matter what she does. Ages 5-8.

Jampolsky, G., and Cirincione, D. (1991). *"Me First" and the Gimme Gimmes.* Deerfield Beach, FL: Health Communication, Inc. A story that shows the transformation of selfishness into love. All ages.

Kaufman, Gershen, and Lev, Raphael. (1990). *Stick Up for Yourself.* Minneapolis, MN: Free Spirit Publishing Co. A guide to help kids feel personal power and self-esteem. Ages 8-12.

Marcus, Irene, and Marcus, Paul. (1990). *Scary Night Visitors.* New York, NY: Magination Press. Davey has fears at night and learns to feel safe through experiencing his feelings directly. Ages 4-7.

Moser, Adolph. (1988). *Don't Pop Your Cork on Monday.* Kansas City, MO: Landmark Editions. A handbook for children to explore the causes of stress and techniques to deal with it. Ages 5-8.

Moser, Adolph. (1991). *Don't Feed the Monster on Tuesday.* Kansas City, MO: Landmark Editions. Dr. Moser offers children information on the importance of knowing their own self-worth and ways to improve self-esteem. Ages 5-8.

Munsch, R., and Martchenko, M. (1985). *Thomas's Snowsuit.* Ontario, Canada: Annick Press Ltd. A story about a child who refuses to wear his snowsuit and will not be manipulated by adults. Ages 5-8.

Oram, Hiawyn. (1982). *Angry Arthur.* New York, NY: E.P. Dutton. Arthur becomes enraged with his mom and creates havoc on the planet. Ages 5-8.

Sanford, Doris, (1986). *Don't Look at Me.* Portland, OR: Multnomah Press. The story of Patrick who feels very stupid and learns to feel special about himself. Ages 7-11.

Seuss, Dr. (1990). *Oh, the Places You'll Go.* New York, NY: Random House. Dr. Seuss uses his magical creativity to inspire young and old to succeed in life, despite the many ups and downs they face. Ages 5-adult.

Simon, Norma. (1989). *I Am Not a Crybaby.* New York, NY: Puffin Books. This book shows how children of different races and cultures share the commonality of feelings. Ages 5-8.

Steig, William. (1988). *Spinky Sulks.* Singapore: Sunburst Books. Spinky is angry and begins to sulk. No one can make him stop until he is ready. Ages 5-8.

Voirst, Judith. (1972). *Alexander and the Terrible Horrible No Good Very Bad Day.* New York, NY: Aladdin Books. Alexander has a day where everything goes wrong. Everyone can relate to this. Ages 5-8.

BOOKS ABOUT NEW SIBLINGS

Alexander, Martha. (1971). *Nobody Asked Me if I Wanted a Baby Sister.* New York, NY: Dial Books. A little boy tries to give his new baby sister away until he realizes she really likes him. Ages 4-7.

Alexander, Martha. (1979). *When the New Baby Comes, I'm Moving Out.* New York, NY: Dial Books. A little boy is angry with his mom for preparing for a new baby. Ages 4-7.

Blume, Judy. (1980). *Superfudge.* New York, NY: Dell Publishing. Peter, a sixth grade boy, learns his mom is having a baby andBoyd, Lizi. (1990). *Sam Is My Half Brother.*wonders how he will survive it. A good book for kids in grades 3 to 7. New York, NY: Puffin Books. Hessie is afraid that her new half brother Sam will get all the love and attention. This book stimulates discussion on stepfamilies. Ages 4-8.

BOOKS ABOUT GOOD-BYES

Brillhart, Julie. (1990). *Anna's Goodbye Apron.* Niles, IL: Albert Whitman and Co. A story about how a kindergarten class says good-bye to their wonderful teacher Anna who has to move. Ages 4-7.

Osborne, Judy. (1978). *My Teacher Said GOODBYE Today.* Brookline, MA: Emijo Press. This story shows how the end of the year when kids and teachers need to say good-bye can evoke lots of feelings. Ages 4-6.

Viorst, Judith. (1992). *The Good-Bye Book.* New York, NY: Aladdin Books. The story of a young child who doesn't want to be left with the baby-sitter. Ages 4-7.

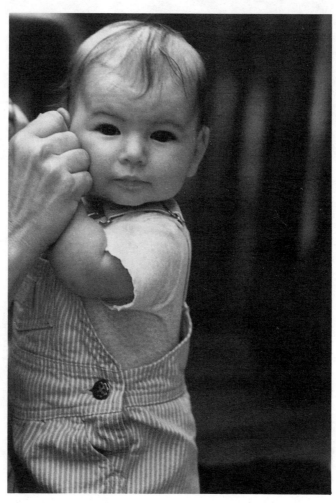

ON CHILDREN

Your children are not your children/They are the sons and daughters of life's longing for itself...

You are the bows from which your children as living arrows are sent forth.

From *The Prophet*, by Kahlil Gibran

(The Prophet—Kahlil Gibran, 1951. New York, NY: Alfred A. Knopf, Inc., Publishers. Copyright renewed by Administrators C.T.A. of Kahlil Gibran estate, Mary G. Gibran. Reprinted with permission.)

REFERENCES

Adams, Caren, and Fay, Jennifer. (1992). *Helping Your Child Recover from Sexual Abuse*. Seattle, WA: University of Washington Press.

Berry, Joy. (1990). *About Change and Moving*. Chicago, IL: Children's Press.

Berry, Joy. (1990). *About Traumatic Experiences*. Chicago, IL: Children's Press.

Blackburn, Lynn. (1991). *I Know I Made It Happen*. Omaha, NE: Centering Corporation.

Bloomfield, Harold, & Felder, Leonard. (1986). *Achilles Syndrome*. New York: Random House.

Buscaglia, Leo. (1982). *The Fall of Freddie the Leaf*. Thorofare, NJ: Charles B. Slack Co.

Cappacchione, Lucia. (1982). *The Creative Journal for Children*. Boston, MA: Shambhala Publishing, Inc.

Carr, Richard. (1973). *Be a Bird, Be a Frog, Be a Tree*. Garden City, NJ: Doubleday & Co., Inc.

Cohen, Miriam. (1984). *Jim's Dog Muffin*. New York, NY: Dell Publishing.

Davis, Diane. (1984). *Something Is Wrong in My House*. Seattle, WA: Parenting Press, Inc.

De Milleis, Richard. (1973). *Put Your Mother on the Ceiling*. New York, NY: Penguin Books.

Doleski, Teddi. (1983). *The Hurt*. Mahwah, NJ: Paulest Press.

Eberling, Carol, & Eberling, David. (1991). *When Grief Comes to School*. Bloomington, IN: Blooming Educational Enterprises.

Fassler, David, Lash, Michele, & Ives, Sally. (1988). *Changing Families*. Burlington, VT: Waterfront Books.

Ferguson, Dorothy. (1992). *A Bunch of Balloons*. Omaha, NE: Centering Corporation.

Fox, Sandra. (1988). *Good Grief: Helping Groups of Children When a Friend Dies*. Boston, MA: New England Association for the Education of Young Children.

Gibran, Kahlil. (1951). *The Prophet*. New York: Alfred A. Knopf, Publishers. Copyright renewed by Administrators C.T.A. of Kahlil Gibran estate.

Heegaard, Marge. (1988). *When Someone Very Special Dies*. Minneapolis, MN: Woodland Press.

Heegaard, Marge. (1990). *When Mom and Dad Separate*. Minneapolis, MN: Woodland Press.

Heegaard, Marge. (1991). *When Someone Has a Very Serious Illness*. Minneapolis, MN: Woodland Press.

Hoban, Tana. (1971). *Look Again*. New York, NY: Macmillian Publishing Co.

Ives, Sally, Fassler, David, & Lash, Michele. (1985). *The Divorce Workbook: A Guide for Kids & Families*. Burlington, VT: Waterfront Books.

Jackson, Edgar. (1973). *Coping with the Crises in Your Life*. Northvale, NJ: Aronson, Jason Inc.

Kubler-Ross, Elisabeth. (Ed.). (1975). *Death: The Final Stage of Growth*. Englewood Cliffs, NJ: Prentice-Hall, Inc.

Lombardo, Victor S., & Lombardo, Edith. (1986). *Kids Grieve Too*. Springfield, IL: C. C. Thomas.

Mellonie, Bryan, & Ingpen, Robert. (1983). *Lifetimes: The Beautiful Way to Explain Death to Children*. New York, NY: Bantam books.

Moser, Adolph. (1988). *Don't Pop Your Cork on Monday*. Kansas City, MO: Landmark Editions.

Oaklander, Violet. (1969). *Windows to Our Children: Gestalt Therapy for Children*. New York, NY: Center for Gestalt Development.

O'Toole, Donna. (1989). *Growing through Grief: A K-12 Curriculum to HELP Young People through All Kinds of Loss*. Burnsville, NC: Mt Rainbow Publications.

Quinlin, Patricia. (1987). *My Daddy Takes Care of Me*. Ontario, Canada: Annick Press.

Rogers, Fred. (1988). *When a Pet Dies*. New York: G.P. Putnam's Sons.

Rubenstein, Judith. (May 14, 1982). Preparing a Child for a Good-bye Visit to a Dying Loved One. *Journal of the American Medical Association* (JAMA), *247*, 2571-72.

Sanford, Doris. (1985a). *It Must Hurt a Lot*. Portland, OR: Multnomah Press.

Sanford, Doris. (1985b). *Please Come Home.* Portland, OR: Multnomah Press.

Sanford, Doris. (1986). *I Can't Talk about It.* Portland, OR: Questar Publishers, Multnomah Press.

Siverstein, Shel. (1974). *Where the Sidewalk Ends.* New York, NY: HarperCollins Publishers.

Stein, Sarah. (1974). *About Dying.* New York, NY: Walker and Co.

Trout, Susan. (1990). *To See Differently.* Washington, DC: Three Roses Press.

Viorst, Judith. (1972). *Alexander and the Terrible Horrible No Good Very Bad Day.* New York, NY: Aladdin Books.

Viorst, Judith. (1992). *The Good-Bye Book.* New York, NY: Aladdin Books.

Weiner, Lori. (September, 1991). Women and Human Immunodeficiency Virus: A historical and personal psychosocial perspective. *Social Work*, 36 (5), 375-378.

White, E.B. (1952). *Charlotte's Web.* New York, NY: Harper and Row.

Wolfelt, Alan. (1983). *Helping Children Cope with Grief.* Muncie, IN: Accelerated Development Inc.

Wolfelt, Alan. (Summer 1992). *Centerpiece* newsletter. Fort Collins, CO: The Center for Loss and Life Transition.

INDEX

INDEX

Grollman, E. 116
Gryte, M. 124
Guilt 60

H

Haasl, B. 126
Habits
    loss of 17-8
Hammond, J. 126
Hastings, J. 134
Hausherr, R. 130
Hazen, B. 135
Heavilin, M. 116
Heegaard, M. 79, 127, 129, 132, 140
Help
    parents seeking 102
    professional 101-3
    ways to make a difference 103
Hickman, M. 134
Hoban, T. 23, 127, 140
Holden. L. 126
Hospice Education Institute 108
Hospice of Northern VA 111
Howard County Sexual Assault Center 111
Huntley, T. 116

I

Ilse, S. 116
Imagination 76
Ingpen, R. 93, 94, 127, 140
Institute for Attitudinal Studies 111
Inventory checklist
    for referral 97-100
Ives, S. 79, 132, 139, 140

J

Jackson, E. 89, 140
Jampolsky, G. 135
Janover, C. 135
Johnson, J. 124
Johnson, M. 124
Johnson, S. 116
Jordan, M. 130
Jordan-Wong, J. 132
Just for Kids The Family Life Center 111

K

Kaldhol, M. 125
Kaufman, G. 135
Kids
    today's problems 2
Kirsch, A. 95
Kolf, J.C. 121
Krementz, J. 123, 132
Kubler-Ross, E. 36, 47, 117, 125, 129, 140
Kushner, H. 117
Kussman, L. 120

L

Lagorio, J. 120
Lanton, S. 123
Lash, M. 79, 132, 139, 140
Lawrence, M. 129
Leon, I. 117
LeShan, E. 123, 129
Letters to loved ones 64-8
Lev, R. 135
Levine, J. 123
Levine, S. 117
Linn, E. 117, 124
Lombardo, E. 3, 140
Lombardo, V. 3, 140
Loss in the environment 8
    help for 9
Loss of external objects
    help for 7
Loss of relationships 5
    help for 6
Loss of self 10
Loss related to habits 17-8
    help for 18
Loss related to skills and abilities 15
    help for 15

M

Manuals
    for adult resources 120
Maple, M. 129
Marcus, I. 135
Marcus, P. 135
Marnocha, J. 126
Martchenko, M. 136
Maryland Committee for Children (The) 111
Materials 113-38
McKend, H. 131
Medical Illness Counseling Center 111
Mellonie, B. 93, 94, 127, 140
Memory books 70-5
Memory boxes 78
Merrifield, M. 131
Miles, M. 128
Miller, A. 117
Mills, G. 117
Mize, Edith 36, 47
Molnar, D. 134
Montgomery County Hospice 111
Montgomery, H. 122
Montgomery, M. 122
Moser, A. 18, 136, 140
Mothers Against Drunk Driving (MADD) 108
Mourning
    definition 21
    relation to grief 21
Moustakas, C. 117
Mulder, L. 131
Munsch, R. 127, 136
Music 79
My Friend's House 112

ABOUT

THE

AUTHOR

Linda Goldman

Having worked as a kindergarten, first- and second-grade teacher, and guidance counselor in the public school for 18 years, I was frustrated with the lack of time and practical information allotted for children in which to learn life as well as studies. This frustration led me into the field of guidance, hoping to create a nurturing environment in which children could explore and express their feelings.

My own personal issues of loss and grief, divorce, miscarriage, and a stillborn daughter, Jennifer, deepened my understanding. My best friend's battle with cancer led me on a frantic search for any available information to help parents and children cope with serious illness. There was little. The Kubler-Ross Foundation was a valuable resource for learning. I participated in a five-day Loss and Grief Workshop in July, 1991, seeing firsthand

how children's losses, not grieved, remained buried as adults.

I began networking all over the country to gather data to create Children's Workshops. I felt strongly there was a void in our educational system and hoped that a changing awareness could fill it. I understood that issues may differ from generation to generation, but the underlying stress, loss, grief, anger, and pain are universal and timeless.

I am now living in Chevy Chase, Maryland, with my husband, Michael, and my son, Jonathan, age seven. I have joined Ellen S. Zinner, a psychologist and past president of the Association for Death Education and Counseling, in creating The Center for Loss and Grief Therapy in Kensington, Maryland. Educating parents, teachers, counselors, and other caring adults is achieved through educational workshops on children's issues of loss and grief, as well as facilitation in ongoing children's bereavement groups.